The Toddler's BUSY BOOK

Trish Kuffner

Ⓜ Meadowbrook Press

Distributed by Simon & Schuster
New York

Library of Congress Cataloging-in-Publication Data
Kuffner, Trish.
    The toddler's busy book / [by Trish Kuffner; illustrations, Laurel Aiello].
    p. cm.
    Includes bibliographical references (p.   ) and index.
    ISBN 0-88166-357-3 (Meadowbrook)—ISBN 0-671-31774-1 (Simon & Schuster)
    1. Creative activities and seat work. 2. Toddlers. I. Title.
    LB1140.35.C74 K845   1999
    372.5—dc21   99-37931
                                                                 CIP

Editors: Liya Lev Oertel, Christine Zuchora-Walske
Copyeditor: Joseph Gredler
Production Manager: Joe Gagne
Desktop Publishing: Danielle White
Cover Art: Dorothy Stott
Illustrations: Laurel Aiello

© 1999 by Patricia Kuffner

Published by Meadowbrook Press, 5451 Smetana Drive, Minnetonka,
Minnesota 55343

www.meadowbrookpress.com

BOOK TRADE DISTRIBUTION by Simon & Schuster, a division of Simon and
Schuster, Inc., 1230 Avenue of the Americas, New York, NY 10020

04 03   13 12 11 10 9

Printed in the United States of America

Acknowledgments

Writing a book while homeschooling three children, chasing a toddler, and struggling through the early months of pregnancy was not an easy job, and I could not have done it without the help of some wonderful people.

First and foremost, I thank God for His love, mercy, and grace, for His leading in my life, and for the daily strength He gives me to meet the many challenges of parenting.

I sincerely thank my mother, Irene McGeorge, my mother-in-law, Betty Kuffner, and my friend, Joy Francescini, who have been so willing this past year to care for my children when I have needed time to write. I am so grateful for the help you have given me.

To my husband, Wayne, and our children Andria, Emily, Joshua, and Johanna, I thank you for being willing to put up with grilled cheese sandwich dinners, an absence of clean clothes, and Saturdays without Mom. I really appreciate the sacrifices you've all made.

Finally, to my editor, Liya Lev Oertel, and my publisher, Bruce Lansky, at Meadowbrook Press, thank you for envisioning *The Toddler's Busy Book* and giving me the opportunity to write it. Your support of my efforts encourages me to continue on this road called writing.

Dedication

For Johanna, our toddler-in-residence.
Writing this book with you was difficult;
without you it would have been impossible.

Contents

Introduction

"Children are the anchors that hold a mother to life."
—*Sophocles*

I began writing *The Toddler's Busy Book* just as my fourth child, Johanna, was entering the toddler stage. She began to walk, then run, several months short of her first birthday, and she hasn't stopped since! After surviving the baby/toddler/preschooler challenge three times with Johanna's older siblings, I'd forgotten what a trial one little toddler can be, especially an extremely active one!

But what a joy it was, too, to watch her grow and develop through the various stages of toddlerhood. Before learning to crawl and walk, she was obliged to sit wherever we put her. Now, only months later, she roams the house at will. What a treat it is to watch her as she teases her siblings and mimics her parents, to see the beginnings of imaginative play as she cuddles her "baby," to notice the emerging concern she shows for others who are crying, and to observe the development of a giving spirit as she shares her cookie with the family cat!

Toddlerhood is a precious stage in the life of both parent and child, and one which can be enjoyed immensely if you are prepared to slow down a little, sit on the floor a lot, and worry about picking up the toys only when your child goes to bed at night. Organize your home to be a safe and interesting place for your child to explore and discover, and introduce your child to new people, places, and experiences as often as you can. Be adventurous and look at life through your child's eyes as she begins to unearth some of the many wonders of this amazing world in which we live.

The Toddler's Busy Book is intended to help you enjoy your child's toddler years. It will help you entertain and stimulate your child through the toddler years with ideas simple and straightforward enough for even the busiest of parents or caregivers to manage. This book contains suggestions for many situations and occasions: for indoors and outdoors, for summer and winter, for quiet times and active times. I've written this book as a resource for parents at home with their toddlers, but it is well-suited for anyone who has a toddler in his or her life: mothers, fathers, grandparents, aunts, uncles, babysitters, day-care providers, preschool teachers, church workers, or playgroup leaders. If you spend any time at all with a toddler, then this book is for you.

Although many of the ideas in *The Toddler's Busy Book* may continue to entertain your child long after the toddler stage, these activities are most suitable for children between the ages of one and three. Because abilities of children in that age range vary greatly, some ideas will be too advanced for a one-year-old, while others will be much too simple for a three-year-old. Use your judgment in choosing activities that best meet the capabilities and interests of your child. If a new activity doesn't go over quite as well as you expected, don't write it off altogether; try it again in a week, a month, or a year, or vary the activity in a way that will make it more meaningful and interesting for your child.

As my oldest child, my very first baby, approaches adolescence, it is a special joy to experience the toddler years again. Having several children halfway to adulthood has given me an appreciation of the brevity of the very early years of childhood—an appreciation I didn't have ten years ago when my oldest was a toddler. Although back then it seemed as though my babies would never grow up, most of them have—and yours will, too. Diapers will one day be a thing of the past, as will bottles, soothers, a bathtub full of toys, afternoon naps, sticky fingers, wet kisses, and so many other earmarks of toddlerhood.

Each stage of childhood brings with it its own set of challenges as well as its own special rewards. Some days will bring you more joy than you ever thought possible, while on other days you'll feel grateful if you (or your children) make it through in one piece. This pattern doesn't change, no matter how old your children are! My hope is that you will love your child unconditionally, remember your sense of humor, and relish the toddler years, because like the fingerprints on the wall, they will be gone before you know it.

Trish

Trish Kuffner

P.S. A note on the use of "his" and "her": In recognition of the fact that children do indeed come in both sexes, and in an effort to represent each, the use of male and female pronouns will alternate with each chapter.

CHAPTER 1

Help! I Have a Toddler!

"A toddler, according to the dictionary, is one who toddles, which means 'to walk with short tottering steps.' Regardless of what the experts or the outsiders say, those tiny steps will plunge you into one of the most exasperating periods of your adult life."
—*Jain Sherrard*

Toddlers may be described in many ways. Some call them terrible (as in "terrible twos"); others call them "terrific" (although I suspect those people do not currently have toddlers in their lives). Most toddlers fall somewhere in between. They are wonderful little people some days and trials on other days.

Toddlers are at an interesting stage of development. They can get around on their own, but they need constant supervision. They understand most of what they hear but are usually unable to communicate their wants and needs effectively. They want to do everything for themselves, but their skills and abilities are limited. They want to try everything, and most of what they do is motivated by an interest in cause and effect. ("Let's see what happens when. . . .")

Toddlers also have an abundance of energy. As they enter the toddler stage, some will still be taking two naps per day, but by the end of toddlerhood, many will not be napping at all. This means that a parent or caregiver must occupy the toddler for many hours each day, often without a break. This can be a challenge for most adults, whether they are encountering life with a toddler for the first time or experiencing toddlerhood for the second, third, or fourth time.

In addition to their abundant energy and desire to learn about the world around them, toddlers also have specific needs and characteristics unique to their stage of development. They are not walking babies or watered-down preschoolers. Expecting them to stay involved in activities that are not sufficiently stimulating or are too advanced for their abilities will lead to frustration for the child and the parent or caregiver.

What, then, do toddlers need? What activities can a parent or caregiver easily provide that will keep a toddler happy, occupied, and stimulated? Parenting an infant is one thing, but coping with the specific needs of a toddler is something many of us find extremely challenging. Parents at home all day—every day—with toddlers often entertain the thought that professionals (early childhood educators or trained and experienced day-care workers) could do a better job of occupying and stimulating their children.

Would your child be happier, better occupied, and more stimulated if he were cared for by professionals? In certain extreme situations, the answer may be yes, but most parents lack only experience and confidence. Whether they know it or not, parents usually have what it takes to keep their toddlers happy and stimulated. Keep in mind that most of the activities in preschools and day-care centers imitate what can naturally occur in the home on a day-to-day basis: talking, singing, reading, exploring, having a snack, playing outdoors, playing with friends or siblings, napping, and so on. Some may feel that the group setting of a preschool or day care will benefit their child, but toddlers do not learn well, if at all, in group situations. Cynthia Catlin, in her book *Toddlers Together: The Complete Planning Guide for a Toddler Curriculum* (Gryphon House, 1994), says, "Toddlers learn best through their independent explorations and interactions with their caregivers, who can promote their learning by initiating activities based on the children's play behaviors and interest."

This means parents and caregivers are instinctively doing things that stimulate their children to learn. Talking on a toy telephone, asking "Where are your ears?" as you change your toddler, playing hide-and-seek or peek-a-boo, letting him bang about with pots and pans in the kitchen—these are activities you've done countless times without thinking you're providing a rich learning environment. You are. Running, sliding, swinging, and playing outside are activities which encourage physical development. Playing with playdough, paints, and crayons develops fine motor skills and promotes creativity. Washing hands before meals teaches health. "Hot! Don't touch!" teaches safety, and a short playtime with friends helps your child learn social skills.

Simply put, toddlers need a stimulating environment and a variety of experiences to help them develop. Activities which emphasize the senses and physical activity will be the most successful. A consistent daily schedule will help your child know what to expect and help him become more independent. He will enjoy repetition of the familiar in songs, books, arts and crafts, and simple games, and he will also be interested in anything new. Try to make a short walk or some outdoor play a part of every day. Be sure to allow your child plenty of free time with interesting things to discover and explore. We all learn best when our interest motivates us to find out about something, and toddlers are no exception.

Don't rely exclusively on books like this to provide fun ideas for your toddler. Many ideas that work for others will not work for your child, or they may not work right now. Watch your child, note what interests him, and go from there. Develop your own file or notebook of activities that interest your child. Some may be variations of the same activity, while others will be entirely new. Children under the age of three master skills through repetition. If something works for you, do it over and over and over again. If your child shows no interest in an activity, stop for a time and try it again in a week, month, or year.

ORGANIZING FOR A TODDLER

In many cases, toddlers know how to create their own fun when given the proper materials. Although they require constant supervision, there are things you can do and materials you can provide that will encourage creative and independent play. The first step is to make sure your home is properly toddler-proofed for safety. Many small items interesting to toddlers, such as coins and beads, pose an extreme choking hazard. Make sure such items are well out of reach—an especially difficult task if you have older children in the house, too.

The following suggestions will help you better organize your home to meet your toddler's changing needs. If you have read *The Preschooler's Busy Book,* you may recognize some of these ideas (modified for toddlers, of course).

Keep a Baker's Box in the kitchen.
Performing kitchen tasks can be extremely difficult when combined with keeping an eye on an energetic toddler. At times, a one-year-old may be happy just to sit in his highchair or at his own little table with a few toys or snacks to keep him occupied while you work. At other times, he will want to be right there with you, underfoot and into everything. Kitchen cupboards and drawers are full of interesting things that may prove irresistible to your child.

Why not provide your child with his very own Baker's Box? Put together a collection of unbreakable kitchen tools in a plastic crate or small storage box. Store it in a spare cupboard that is low enough for your child to reach. He can use his tools for play or for helping you do some "real" cooking or baking. Some suggestions for a Baker's Box are:

cake pan

cake rack

cookie cutters

cookie sheet

large metal or

plastic bowl

measuring spoons

muffin tin

pie plate

plastic measuring cups

rubber spatula

wooden spoon

Have a Busy Box handy.

Since much of our time at home is spent in the kitchen, a spare kitchen cupboard low enough for your child to reach is an ideal spot for his very own Busy Box—a small storage box or plastic crate containing things he can do on his own anytime. An older toddler or preschooler will appreciate many craft supplies in his Busy Box: crayons, markers, coloring books, paper, tape, stickers, scissors, glue, ink pad and stamps, playdough, and so on. But filling a Busy Box for a younger toddler is more of a challenge. Most of us don't want our one-year-olds into tape and markers without close supervision.

Items for a toddler's Busy Box must be safe enough for him to play with relatively unsupervised, and they should be things that will not make a mess (at least not much of a mess). Watch what types of things interest your toddler and include those in his Busy Box. For example, if he loves playing with plastic bottles and lids, put some in the box (be sure the lids are big enough to pass the choke test). Most toddlers love to build, so add an assortment of stackable things. Items that work well are empty cereal boxes, thread spools, covered yogurt containers, and individually wrapped rolls of toilet paper.

Many ideas in this book are suitable for your toddler's Busy Box. In Chapter 2, for example, you will find Sticky Figures, Texture Touch, Surprise Tins, Shaker Bottle, Who Do You See?, Mailbox, Wave Bottle, Bubble Bottle, Clothespin Drop, Clothespin Poke, Grocery Store, What's in the Jar?, Fun with Kleenex, and Squishy Bag.

While most children have favorite things they like to play with, something new to discover and explore will hold their attention and keep them occupied. If you vary the contents of the Busy Box from day to day, your toddler will always find something fresh and exciting to keep him busy and happy.

Set up a Tickle Trunk.

A Tickle Trunk full of dress-up clothes and props will not only foster your child's imaginative play but will keep him occupied with all the wonders it contains. Fill a trunk, toy box, large plastic container, or cardboard box with adult clothes, shoes, hats, scarves, gloves, and costume jewelry to use for dress-up. Old suits are great, as are Hawaiian shirts, vests, baseball hats, bridesmaid dresses, nightgowns, wigs, boots, slippers, and purses. Great items can be found at garage sales or local thrift shops, or stock up on princess gowns and animal costumes at post-Halloween sales.

A toddler may have trouble with zippers and small buttons, so consider replacing them with Velcro or enlarging the buttonholes and replacing small buttons with large ones that are easy for little fingers to grasp.

Investing in a Tickle Trunk full of dress-up clothes may well be one of the best toys you can assemble for your toddler. Not only will it help keep him busy and happy during his early years, but chances are it will become an invaluable part of his play for many years to come.

Make up a Rainy Day Box.

Although all days with babies, toddlers, and preschoolers can seem long, rainy days seem to have extra hours to fill. When the weather is bad or when your child is sick, a Rainy Day Box full of surprises can help break the monotony. Good things to put in your Rainy Day Box are:

- Fresh, new art supplies (a new pad, markers, paintbox, stickers, or playdough).
- A new toy (or one that hasn't been played with in a while).
- A new book, music tape, or video.
- Special dress-up items.
- Cookie cutters and a new or favorite cookie recipe.
- Supplies and directions for a new game or craft (preassemble all supplies and store them in a Ziploc bag in the Rainy Day Box until ready to use).

Don't overuse your Rainy Day Box. It will be regarded with interest and awe only if its appearance is somewhat extraordinary. Store your Rainy Day Box in a safe place and bring it out only when the day seems unusually long.

Make a Job Jar for your child.

Whether you're working a full-time job or staying home with your child, whether you're a day-care provider or an occasional babysitter, there will be times when chores need to be done with your toddler close by. Instilling a sense of responsibility toward household chores is something that can be started at this tender age. (Even very young toddlers like to feel they're helping.)

You can make a Job Jar out of an empty jar, coffee can, or small box. Cut strips of paper and print a small job that needs to be done on each one. Very young toddlers will enjoy wiping the floor or refrigerator with a damp cloth or sponge, stacking towels in a cupboard, or picking up toys and placing them in a basket or container. You will know the jobs your child is capable of doing with minimum supervision and assistance.

Rotate your child's toys.

In the first few years of life, most children receive many wonderful toys as gifts for birthdays, holidays, or other occasions. While parents appreciate the good intentions of the givers, most children have more toys than they can possibly play with. Also, even the most creative toys will fail to hold your child's interest if they're always around. When rotated every four to six weeks, toys will seem new to him and will be interesting and exciting all over again.

Separate your child's toys into piles. (If your child has a favorite toy, keep it out all the time.) Keep one pile in your child's play area and pack the others away in boxes, marking dates for when they are to be brought out. If you have friends with children the same age, why not try a toy exchange? Keep a list of what's been exchanged and be sure to agree on the terms beforehand (how long, who's responsible for breakage, and so on).

Make a Crazy Can.

Someone once referred to the dinner hour as "arsenic hour." Once you've had a toddler or two hanging around at that time, you'll know why! This is usually the time when you are at your busiest and toddlers are at their crankiest. In the midst of the chaos, you yearn for a distraction to keep them busy. It's not a great time to brainstorm for creative activities, so plan ahead with a Crazy Can full of ideas for your toddler.

Make a list of on-the-spot activities that require no special materials, no time-consuming preparation or cleanup, and no serious adult participation or supervision. Write these ideas down on index cards or small pieces of paper and put them in an empty coffee can. If you like, cover the can with cheerful contact paper, or cover it with plain paper and have your child decorate it with paints, markers, or crayons. When things start to get crazy (or when there's just nothing to do), choose a card from the can for an instant remedy. Appendix B on page 365 offers a list of activities appropriate for a toddler Crazy Can.

Take along a Busy Bag.

A Busy Bag will help you be prepared for those times when you have to wait at the doctor's office, hairdresser's, or restaurant. Turn a drawstring bag or backpack into a take-along Busy Bag that can be filled with special goodies to keep your child amused. Borrow the portable items from your Busy Box, or take along items such as:

- Dolls and their associated clothing, blankets, bottles, and accessories.
- An edible necklace (like cereal or crackers with holes in the middle strung on a piece of shoestring licorice).
- A favorite toy, stuffed animal, or blanket.
- Magnets and a small metal cake pan.
- Matchbox cars.
- Simple wooden puzzles.
- Special snacks.
- Stickers and a sticker book or plain notebook.

Use your imagination when filling the Busy Bag. You can assemble it by yourself so the contents will be a surprise for your child, or you can have your child help you fill the bag before you go. Chapter 6 contains many ideas that will help keep your toddler happy and busy when you're out and about.

Look for new activities and experiences.
While children need free time for creative play and unstructured time in which to explore the world around them, they also rely on you to introduce them to new projects, activities, and adventures. This is sometimes hard to do on the spur of the moment, so planning ahead is a good idea. Try to schedule one or two fun, challenging, creative activities each day (not necessarily major projects—sometimes a five-minute game will do). Decide on the activities ahead of time and assemble all the necessary supplies in advance.

PLANNING YOUR ACTIVITIES

As I mentioned in *The Preschooler's Busy Book,* failing to plan is planning to fail. That applies to the big stuff (like saving for your child's education) as well as the little stuff (like doing a new art project or playing a game with your child). Preschools and day cares plan their curricula carefully to ensure that children have a wide variety of experiences each day. Parents at home can be somewhat less structured, but the importance of planning new and creative activities should not be overlooked. Children's activity books and resources abound and can be easily purchased or borrowed from the local library. However, the ideas in these books are only valuable if you use them. If you don't do a little planning, chances are you won't use them. Here are some helpful guidelines for planning your activities:

1. Read this book from cover to cover and create a weekly planner with activities you'd like to try each day. (Use a copy of the Weekly Activity Planner on page 20.) Include a few alternate activities for bad-weather days or for when your planned activities just won't work.
2. Use your weekly activity plan to make a list of supplies you'll need, and assemble or purchase them beforehand.
3. Make a list of what you need to prepare before your child becomes involved in the activity. Mix paint, assemble supplies, and so on.
4. Plan special activities for your babysitter and have all the necessary materials handy. This will let your sitter know that watching TV all day is not an option.
5. Make a list of ideas that would be fun to do anytime you can fit them into your schedule. Have this list ready when you have some unexpected free time.

STOCKING YOUR CRAFT CUPBOARD

Most of the activities in this book require some basic supplies. Whether you use an actual cupboard or just a box in the basement, following are some of the items you'll need to stock your craft cupboard.

Things to save:

aluminum foil
aluminum pie plates (various sizes)
balls (golf, Ping-Pong, tennis)
berry baskets
bottle caps
boxes
bubble wrap
buttons
candles
canning rings
cardboard
catalogs
cereal and pasta (dry)
cereal boxes
chopsticks
clean, empty food cans
coffee cans with lids
coffee filters
coins
confetti
containers with handles
corks
cotton balls
cotton batting
cotton swabs
diaper-wipe containers
dried beans
dried pasta (different shapes and sizes)
dried-up markers
egg cartons
eggshells
envelopes
fabric scraps
feathers
felt
film canisters
greeting cards (used)
jars and lids (empty)
junk mail
large, light objects to lift and carry
lids of all kinds
magazines
metal cookie tins
metal lids from frozen juice cans
milk cartons (all sizes)
newspapers
old calendars
old clothes and costume jewelry for dress-up
old magazines
old mittens, socks, and gloves for puppets
old sheets
old telephone books
old toothbrushes
paint sample chips

paper bags (all
    sizes)
paper clips
paper muffin cup
    liners
paper plates/cups/
    bowls
paper scraps
paper towel/toilet
    paper tubes
photographs of
    friends and
    family
pine cones
plastic bowls, lids,
    and bottles
plastic milk jugs
plastic yogurt and
    margarine con-
    tainers

popcorn
Popsicle sticks
ribbon scraps
rice (uncooked)
rocks
roll-on deodorant
    bottles (empty)
rubber bands
salt shakers or
    spice containers
    (empty)
sandpaper
scarves (chiffon-
    type)
shells
shoeboxes with
    lids
shoelaces
soda bottles
    (empty)

spray bottle
squeeze bottles
    (the kind mus-
    tard and ketchup
    come in)
stamps
stickers of all
    kinds
string
Styrofoam trays
swizzle sticks
thread
thread spools
tissue paper scraps
toothpicks
wood scraps
wrapping paper
    scraps
yarn scraps

Things to buy:

art smock (or use an old shirt)
balloons
beads (large for toddlers)
bells
chalk
child-safe scissors
clear acrylic spray
contact paper (clear and colored)
clothespins (craft- and spring-type)
colored cellophane
colored tape
construction paper in various colors
craft magnets
crayons

crepe paper
elastic
fabric paint
food coloring
glitter
glue gun
glue or glue sticks
googly eyes
hole punch
index cards
liquid starch
magnet strips
masking tape
newsprint pads or rolls
paper clips
paper doilies
paper fasteners
pencil crayons
pencil sharpener

pencils
pens
pipe cleaners
plain writing pads
plastic Easter eggs
plastic tubing
pompoms
rubber cement
ruler
sponges
stapler
stickers
straws
tempera paints and brushes
tissue paper
transparent tape
washable markers
wooden spoons
Ziploc freezer bags

WHAT ABOUT TELEVISION?

The influence of television on children has been much debated over the years. While your child may still be young enough that television is not yet an issue, be assured that it is something you will need to think about carefully in the months and years to come.

As I stated in *The Preschooler's Busy Book,* the crux of the children-and-television issue is not so much what children watch, because we can control that. I am more concerned about how parents use television and what children do not do when they watch television. It's easy to use television as a babysitter, but TV can be habit-forming to both parent and child. The few short years of early childhood are better spent playing, reading, walking, talking, painting, and crafting—in other words, doing things together.

However, whether we like it or not, television is here to stay. It's up to parents to use it in a way that will be beneficial to their child's development and their parent/child relationship. How should parents do this? First, be selective in what your children watch. Good television programs can make learning fun and can expand your child's knowledge of the world. As your toddler gets older, programs like *Sesame Street* can help him get ready for school. Choose wisely. Look for programs or videotapes which instruct, entertain, and reinforce the values and principles you wish to develop in your child.

Second, limit your child's daily viewing time. Remember, time spent watching TV is time your child does not spend on other more valuable activities such as playing games, reading (or being read to), or using his imagination in countless other ways.

Third, watch TV with your child whenever possible. Most programs move at a very fast pace to hold the attention of their young audience. But young children often have a hard time keeping track of the content, and it is almost impossible for them to stop and ponder what is being presented. By watching with your child, you can provide connections that would otherwise be missed. And by reminding your child of related events in his own life, you can help him make sense of what he sees.

Finally, set an example for your child. Show him that you would rather read a book or play a game or talk to him than watch TV. It's hard to expect your child to limit his viewing and choose programs wisely when you do just the opposite. Remember, children learn more from our actions than our words.

A WORD OF ENCOURAGEMENT

Raising a child is a monumental task which brings countless rewards, most of which will be realized only after many years of hard work. But there are also many "warm fuzzies" you receive daily as a parent: the first time your baby smiles at you, his first word, his first step, his warm hugs, and that irresistably cute thing he did that you can't wait to tell Grandma and Grandpa about. As your child moves through the various stages of early childhood from infant to toddler to preschooler, you will also see the changes that parenting is bringing about in you. You will stretch and grow as a person, you will learn new things (many of them about yourself), and you will develop more patience than you ever thought possible.

If you are parenting a preschooler and a toddler, or a toddler and an infant, or all three (or more) at the same time, the daily challenges you face are even greater. You may not be able to get out as much as you want, or do as many fun and interesting things as you'd like one-on-one with each child, but chances are if you care enough to read a book such as this, you're already doing a great job. Treasure what you've been given, keep a positive outlook on life, and do the best job you can each day. (Your kids will grow up—I promise!)

Is there only one way to raise happy, healthy, confident, and capable children? Of course not. But by providing your child with daily activities that are simple and fun, by placing more importance on your child's happiness and learning than on the appearance of your home, and by talking to your child on a level he understands, you are well on your way to achieving this goal. Not only will he be better prepared for preschool, kindergarten, and the world beyond, but in the process, you'll help to make many happy memories of childhood.

Weekly Activity Planner

Week of:

To Do	To Buy
Monday _____ _____ _____	_____ _____ _____
Tuesday _____ _____ _____	_____ _____ _____
Wednesday _____ _____ _____	_____ _____ _____
Thursday _____ _____ _____	_____ _____ _____

Weekly Activity Planner

Week of:

To Do	To Buy
Friday _____ _____ _____	_____ _____ _____ _____
Saturday _____ _____ _____	_____ _____ _____ _____
Sunday _____ _____ _____	_____ _____ _____ _____
Rainy Day Options _____ _____ _____	_____ _____ _____ _____

CHAPTER 2
Rainy Day Play

A Mother's Prayer:
Dear Lord,

So far today I've done all right. I haven't gossiped, I haven't lost my temper, I haven't been greedy, grumpy, nasty, selfish, or very indulgent. I'm very grateful for that. But in a few minutes, Lord, I'm going to get out of bed, and from then on, I'm going to need a lot more help. Amen.

Most parents of very young children will agree that a bout of rainy weather can try the patience of even the calmest, most tolerant among us. Days seem longer, kids seem crankier, and somehow there never seems to be enough to do to keep our energetic little ones occupied.

The west coast of British Columbia, where we live, is often called "the wet coast." I've had more experience than I'd care to remember dealing with housebound babies, toddlers, and preschoolers. When my three oldest children were young, there were many rainy days when everyone was up at 5 A.M., our entire day's worth of activities was completed by about 8 A.M., and there, stretching before us, were at least eight or nine more hours to fill until Daddy came home.

On days like these that seem especially never-ending, my best advice is to get out of the house, if you possibly can. Call a friend and get together for lunch or a midmorning visit. Dress everyone in rain gear and go out for a short walk. If you live close to a fast-food restaurant with a "play place," take advantage of it. You don't have to spend a lot. Midmornings and afternoons can be quite slow, and owners don't usually mind you playing for an hour or two if you buy coffee or a juice. You can even go to a mall just to walk around and window-shop. We had one with a big indoor fountain close by, and my little girls spent a fair bit of time throwing pennies into it.

But if you can't get out, for whatever reason, be prepared with lots of fun things for your little ones to do indoors. In many instances, children will create their own fun when given the proper materials:

- Put together a collection of things for your toddler to stack: Empty cereal boxes, thread spools, and small yogurt containers with lids work well.
- Give your child a variety of safe, unbreakable kitchen objects so she can make her own symphony: wooden spoons, wire whisks, rubber spatulas, pots and pans with lids, and so on.
- Place a smooth board against a chair or couch to create a ramp to roll things down.
- Help your child create simple puppets out of a paper bag and cardboard tube.

- Don't forget to look in other chapters for more great ideas for indoor fun. Kids in the Kitchen (Chapter 3), Early Learning Fun (Chapter 8), Music and Movement (Chapter 9), and of course Arts and Crafts (Chapter 10) offer countless activities to keep your toddler entertained. While the ideas in this chapter may come in especially handy on rainy days, most are suitable for every day! Many can be easily adapted for outdoor play when the weather is fair.

Inside/Outside Voice

Children are never too young to begin learning consideration for others. Even very young children can be taught this simple rule, and it's a lifesaver on rainy indoor days.

Ask your child, "How many eyes do I have?" "How many ears do I have?" "How many hands do I have?" Go on to explain that we all have two voices, too. One is a great, big, loud voice; the other is a smaller, softer voice. One voice is good for outside, and one voice is good for inside. Ask your child, "Which voice would be good for inside?" and "Which voice are we using now?"

Doll Bed

Large cardboard box
Towels or old receiving blankets
Old baby blanket
Small pillow

Make a bed for your child's doll out of a large cardboard box.
Use towels or old receiving blankets for bedding. Add a small
pillow and a baby blanket if you have one. Your toddler will
enjoy putting her baby to bed and waking her up again.

Tape City

Before taping your floor or carpet, test the tape on a small area to make sure it can be easily removed. Leaving the tape on the floor for more than a day may also make it gummy and difficult to remove.

Masking tape
Small cars

Use masking tape on your floor or carpet to create an indoor roadway for small cars. Very young children will enjoy a simple roadway to run their cars along. Older children may enjoy adding parking lots, shops, and schools or accessorizing with dollhouses, toy people, and plastic animals.

Sheet Day

Sheet Day can become an informal holiday in your house every time you strip the beds to change the sheets.

Bed sheets

Since you're stripping the beds anyway, give your child the sheets from all the beds you're changing. She can use them to create houses, tents, forts, or anything else she can dream up. When playtime is over, help your child gather up the sheets and put them in the laundry basket, then take them to the laundry room together.

Chair Maze

Chairs

This activity will work well outdoors as well as in. Place chairs in a maze around the room. Let your child crawl among them or walk over them, or use them as a train for her stuffed animals.

Sticky Figures

Flat piece of wood
Glue gun
Velcro
Small figures of animals, dinosaurs, cowboys, and so on

Glue Velcro onto a flat piece of wood (use a piece that will fit on the tray of your child's highchair). Glue pieces of Velcro onto the bottom of small figures that your child likes to play with. She may amuse herself for quite a while sticking and unsticking these figures on the piece of wood. This technique could also help older children avoid frustration when scenes they are trying to set up keep falling over.

Texture Touch

Materials of varying textures: sandpaper, old carpeting,
  fabric, cotton balls, fun fur, and so on
Metal lids from frozen-juice cans
Glue
Magnets

Cut the various materials you have gathered into a round
shape that will fit the frozen-juice-can lids. Glue the material
onto the lid. Younger toddlers will enjoy simply feeling the
textures. Magnets glued to the back of the juice lids will allow
your child to play with them on the refrigerator or on a cookie
sheet placed on the tray of her highchair.

  For older children, make two sets and have them sort the
lids by matching the materials or sorting by texture (smooth-
est to roughest, softest to hardest, and so on).

Surprise Tins

Stack up a few of these in the cupboards that your child explores. She will enjoy discovering what's inside.

*Round metal cookie tins with lids (or small shoeboxes with
   lids, or empty diaper-wipe containers)*
*Variety of objects: plastic magnetic letters, baby-food jar lids,
   plastic milk-bottle caps, small blocks, and so on*

Fill several round, metal cookie tins with different objects.
Fill one tin with plastic milk-bottle caps, another with metal
baby-food jar lids, a third with small wooden blocks, and so
on. Stack the tins in a cupboard your child can explore. She
will enjoy taking them out, shaking them, taking the lids off
(maybe with your help), and discovering what's inside. You
can also store things such as Texture Touch (page 31) or
Picture Sort (page 181) in tins or boxes like this.

Ice Cube Bags

Ice cube tray
Water
Red, yellow, and blue food coloring
3 Ziploc bags

Mix water and food coloring (enough for two ice cubes of each color) and pour into an ice cube tray. When frozen, place a red and a yellow ice cube into one Ziploc bag, a red and a blue ice cube into the second Ziploc bag, and a yellow and a blue ice cube into the third Ziploc bag. Younger children will enjoy moving the ice cubes around in the bags, while older children will enjoy watching what happens when the two colors melt together.

Shaker Bottle

Clean, empty 16-ounce soda bottle with cap
Colored rice or pasta
Glue gun or quick-bonding glue

Make sure the soda bottle you are using is clean and dry.
Place colored rice or pasta (see Appendix A for instructions on
how to dye pasta and rice) into the bottle and glue the cap on.
Little ones will love to see what's happening inside as they
shake and rattle their bottle.

Sticky Feet

Clear contact paper
Tape

Cut a piece of clear contact paper at least 2 feet long. Remove
the backing and tape the contact paper, sticky side up, to the
floor or carpeting. Toddlers will have fun running, jumping,
dancing, or just standing on the paper. Not only will their
feet stick to the paper, but lifting them also makes a wonderful sound.

Highchair Fun

Be sure to use string that is not long enough to pose a choking hazard, and never leave your child unattended in her highchair.

Short lengths of string
Small toys

Tie one end of short lengths of string to a few of your child's toys. Tie or tape the other ends to the tray of her highchair. She will enjoy throwing the toys off the highchair tray, then pulling the strings to get them back again.

Who Do You See?

Small plastic mirror
Box with lid
Glue
Colorful contact paper, construction paper, or gift-wrap
  (optional)

Glue a small mirror inside a box. If you like, decorate the outside of the box and lid with colorful contact paper, construction paper, or gift-wrap. Place the lid on top of the box. When your child opens the box, she will see someone special!

If you don't have a small plastic mirror and don't want your child playing with something breakable, try gluing photographs or other pictures to the inside of the box. Use photos of your child, her friends, and her family or pictures of people, animals, or other objects cut from magazines or greeting cards.

Bottles and Lids

Collection of bottles and lids of varying sizes

Save small plastic bottles with screw-type lids. Your toddler will have lots of fun matching lids to bottles, putting the lids on, taking the lids off, and starting all over again. A bottle collection is also great fun for the bath, or for water play outdoors.

Fun with Tape

Simple as it may seem, a small piece of tape can provide young children with a lot of enjoyment. Collect a few different kinds of colorful plastic tape, masking tape, double-sided tape, and so on. Your toddler will sometimes enjoy using tape in place of glue when making a collage.

Pieces of tape

Give your young child one or two pieces of tape to play with. She may try sticking them together, to herself, to you, or to other objects around the house. Be sure to watch her if you're worried about the tape sticking to precious books or papers that may be in her path.

Block Sorter

Shoebox with lid
Wooden blocks (square, cylinder, triangle, and rectangle)
Marker
Scissors

Place the blocks on the shoebox lid and trace around them. Cut around the outline of each shape. Place the lid on the shoebox and give the blocks to your toddler. She will have lots of fun poking the shapes through the holes, opening the lid, retrieving the shapes, and starting over again.

Simple Sorter

If you don't have any Ping-Pong or golf balls handy, try using round plastic milk-jug lids instead.

Ping-Pong or golf balls
Plastic container with lid

Cut a hole big enough for a Ping-Pong or golf ball to fit through in the lid of the plastic container. Place the lid on the container and let your toddler have fun poking the balls through the hole. She will quickly learn how to remove the lid to retrieve the balls, but will need your help to replace the lid on the container so she can start over again.

Threading

Shoelace or thin plastic tubing
Items for threading: empty thread spools, large beads, hair
  curlers, tubular pasta, paper towel tubes cut into 1-inch rings

Collect a variety of round objects such as empty spools, large
beads, plastic hair curlers, large tubular pasta, or paper towel
tubes cut into 1-inch rings. Show your child how to thread
these items onto a shoelace or length of thin plastic tubing. Tie
one of the objects being threaded to the end of the lace or tubing to prevent the rest from slipping off.

Mailbox

Shoebox with lid
Scissors
Unopened junk mail

Cut a large slit in the lid of a shoebox. If you like, cover the
box and lid (separately) with colored paper, or decorate with
paints, markers, and stickers. Place the lid on the box and
show your toddler how to "mail" letters. If you don't mind her
doing so, she may enjoy ripping open the letters as much as
mailing them. Store the mail inside the box when play is over.

Wave Bottle

Clean, empty 16-ounce soda bottle with cap
Water
Food coloring
Glitter, sequins, or beads (optional)
Baby oil
Quick-bonding glue

Fill the clean soda bottle with water to about one-third full. Add a few drops of food coloring and glitter, sequins, or beads (optional), then fill the rest of the bottle with baby oil. Glue the cap securely onto the bottle by applying the glue to the inside of the bottle cap and screwing it on. Your child will enjoy gently shaking the bottle to produce beautiful waves.

Bubble Bottle

Clean, empty 32-ounce soda bottle with cap
Water
Tempera paint
⅓ cup liquid detergent

Fill the clean soda bottle with water to about one-third full.
Add a spoon or two of tempera paint and the liquid detergent.
Glue the cap securely onto the bottle by applying glue to the
inside of the bottle cap and screwing it on. Your child will
enjoy shaking the bottle to make colored bubbles.

For a quick and easy alternative, put small pieces of yarn
(about 3–6 inches long) into a clean, empty soda bottle. Fill
the bottle with water and glue the cap on. Your child will
enjoy shaking the bottle to make the yarn dance.

Ring Fun

Canning rings
Wooden spoon
Playdough (See Appendix A for recipe)
Small plastic container

Fill a small plastic container with playdough and insert a
wooden spoon in the middle. (If you want to keep your child's
fingers out of the playdough, use a container with a lid; cut
a hole in the lid big enough for the wooden spoon to go
through.) Give your child a stack of canning rings and show
her how to place the rings over the end of the wooden spoon.

Clothespin Drop

Clean plastic milk jug with lid (½-gallon or 1-gallon size)
6–8 clothespins

Put the clothespins in the jug and screw on the lid. Your toddler will enjoy shaking the jug with the clothespins inside. Show her how to remove the lid (or do it for her if she can't quite do it on her own), shake the clothespins out, then drop them back in again one by one. For variety, try using a couple of spoons in place of clothespins. They make an interesting sound when the jug is shaken.

Clothespin Can

Craft-type clothespins (without springs)
Empty coffee can

Show your toddler how to place the clothespins around the rim of a coffee can. You can also cut a small hole in the plastic lid of the can and have her drop the clothespins through the hole. She'll like the sound they make as they hit the bottom. Store the clothespins in the covered coffee can when not in use.

Indoor Sandbox

In *The Preschooler's Busy Book,* I suggest making an indoor sandbox by filling up a cardboard box or plastic baby bathtub with puffed wheat or rice cereal or uncooked rice. Here are some alternatives that may be purchased fairly inexpensively in bulk. They provide an interesting sensory experience for toddlers.

water softener salt	*shredded paper*
birdseed	*cedar shavings*
dried beans	*deer corn*
oatmeal	*foam packing peanuts*
cornmeal	*potting soil (if you're brave!)*

Children enjoy playing in the sandbox with cups, spoons, bowls, buckets, scoops, shovels, cars, and other toys and containers. A funnel and scoop that can be used to fill an empty plastic soda bottle with sandbox material will also be a hit. An old sheet, shower curtain, or plastic tablecloth placed under the sandbox makes cleanup a little easier.

Clothespin Poke

Empty egg carton
Clothespins

Turn the egg carton upside down and punch small holes (just big enough to fit the clothespin) in the bottom of each section. Place clothespins in the holes and let your toddler have fun taking them out and putting them back in again.

All Gone!

Two large containers
Basket or small bucket with handle
Small toys

Fill one large container with small toys. Place the empty container across the room or some distance away from the full one. Show your child how to fill her basket with toys from the full container, carry them across the room, and dump them into the empty container. It may take more than one trip to empty the first container, or she may decide to take them back to the first container right away. Whenever a container is empty, say, "All gone!"

Grocery Store

Toddlers have fun filling up bags and baskets with just about anything. For variety, use blocks or Duplo in place of the groceries suggested here.

Paper bag with handles or small basket
Empty food boxes and containers

Save up empty food boxes and containers. Pudding or Jell-O boxes work well, as do cereal boxes, small yogurt containers, and empty vitamin bottles. Seal the boxes with tape, then use a glue gun to permanently attach the lids to the small containers. (They may be a choking hazard.) Store all your "groceries" in a box or laundry basket. Your child will have fun "going shopping" with a paper bag or small basket.

Rock Play

Johanna, my toddler-in-residence while I was writing this book, loved to play with rocks. No matter where we were outside, she was sure to be found playing with rocks. Of course rocks found their way inside, and we found them everywhere: with her toys, in her crib, in the bathtub, and inside cupboards. She never seemed to tire of her little rock collection.

Rocks
Containers
Basket with handle

Take your toddler on a walk outside. Bring along a plastic bucket or basket with handle and collect rocks as you walk. Be sure to choose rocks big enough to pass the choke test (or simply discard the smaller ones when you return home). When you get home, wash off the rocks and set them out with some containers for your child to play with. She will enjoy placing them one by one in the containers, dumping them out, carrying them around with her in a basket, and putting them in her pockets or purse. She may also enjoy painting them or placing them in a covered coffee can to make a loud shaker toy.

What's in the Jar?

Toddlers always love taking lids off small containers and jars. It's even more fun when there's an interesting toy inside!

Small clear plastic jars with lids
Small toys that will fit into each jar

Place a small, colorful toy into a clear plastic jar and close the lid. Give your toddler the jar and let her remove the lid and retrieve the toy inside. She'll probably want to do it again and again.

Where's Teddy?

Teddy bear or plush toy
Long string

Tie one end of a long string around one of your child's plush toys or her favorite teddy bear. Hide the bear under a bed or in a closet or drawer. Trail the string from the bear's hiding place around the room, over and under furniture, out the door, and down the hall as far as you like. Give the end of the string to your child and say, "Where's Teddy?" (or use the toy's name). Help her follow the string to find the bear.

Bear in the Basket

What parent hasn't come into a child's room after naptime and discovered every doll, bear, animal, and blanket on the floor? Children won't need much help catching on to this game!

Stuffed animals
Large basket or container

Place a large basket or container next to your child's crib (empty laundry baskets or hampers work well). Place her in the crib along with a teddy bear or supply of stuffed animals or other soft, light toys. Show her how to drop the bear into the basket. You may want to count to her, "One, two, three, drop the bear!"

Fun with Kleenex

Most toddlers have probably tried this on their own at one time or another.

Box of Kleenex

Give your toddler a box of Kleenex and let her pull the Kleenex out one by one. The fun your toddler will have and the time she spends on this will justify the price of the box of Kleenex! If you'd rather not use real Kleenex, stuff a few scarves or pieces of brightly colored tissue paper into an empty Kleenex box and let your child pull those out instead.

Nuts and Bolts

Large nuts and bolts

Purchase several large nuts and bolts and keep them on hand for your older child (probably three and up). She will enjoy screwing nuts on and off the bolts, and you can use this as a counting activity, too.

Nesting Cans

I bought a popular set of twelve nesting cups when my first child was an infant. Ten years later, I don't think anyone (other than myself) has ever put all twelve cups back in order! Three or four cups or cans are sufficient for most toddlers.

3–4 cans that fit inside one another
Duct tape
Scissors
Contact paper or construction paper

Make a set of nesting cans by saving three or four cans that fit inside one another. Make sure there are no sharp edges, then cover the rim of each can with duct tape. Cover each can with contact paper or construction paper. Your child will have fun dumping the cans, then fitting them back together. Turn the cans upside down to build a tower.

For a sorting activity, make two or three sets of nesting cans. Cover each set in a different color or pattern of contact or construction paper.

Toddler Train

Your child will enjoy filling up each car with her stuff and pulling the train behind her wherever she goes.

3 or more assorted boxes
String, ribbon, or yarn
Plastic straws
Scissors

Use scissors or another pointed object to poke small holes in the ends of each box. Insert about 1 foot of string, ribbon, or yarn into the back hole of the first box, then tie the end of the string around a short piece of plastic straw to prevent it from pulling through the hole. Insert the other end of the string through the front hole of the next box and fasten it in the same way. Use more string to continue connecting the boxes until the train is finished. Use a longer length of string for the front hole of the first box. Tie a cylindrical wooden block or small plastic vitamin bottle to the end of this string for a handle.

Pull Box

Small box without lid
Thick rope

Punch a small hole in one end of the small box (a shoebox is ideal). Insert one end of the rope through the hole and tie a knot so that the rope will not pull through the hole. Your child will have fun filling her box with blocks, rocks, small toys, or other objects and pulling it behind her around the room or outside on a walk.

Potty Pals

I've never used this idea myself, but one mom says it's the only thing that helped get her three-year-old out of diapers.

Colorful contact paper
Scissors

Cut out eyes and a smile from contact paper and stick them to the underside of each toilet seat your child will be using. (Don't forget your child's potty, if she has one.) Your child can name the potty pals and assume responsibility for "feeding" them throughout the day. This idea can make going to the potty an exciting event rather than something to avoid.

Blanket Riding

This activity works best on smooth flooring such as hard-wood, linoleum, or ceramic.

Blanket, sheet, or large towel

Sit your child in the middle of a blanket, sheet, or large towel. Grasp the edge of the blanket and gently pull her around the room.

Jungle Safari

This is a great way to get your toddlers and preschoolers to bed at night.

Stuffed animals
Flashlight

Just before bedtime, when pajamas are on and teeth are brushed, hide your child's stuffed animals in odd places around the house (for very young children, you may have to hide them in rather obvious places at first). Turn off the lights and use a flashlight to hunt for the animals hiding in your house.

Nursing Basket

This is a great idea for the toddler who seems to need something every time you sit down to nurse or feed your new baby. This idea also works well when you need to make a few phone calls without interruptions.

Small basket, box, drawstring bag, or plastic
  storage container
Snacks, special toys, books, and so on

Put together a nursing basket for your toddler by assembling a collection of special snacks, toys, books, or other treats that can be brought out only when you nurse the baby. When you're finished nursing or feeding your baby, put the basket away until the next time.

Porcupine Playdough

Playdough (See Appendix A for recipes)
Wooden Popsicle sticks or plastic drinking straws

Give your child a lump of playdough and a bunch of wooden Popsicle sticks or plastic drinking straws. Show her how to poke the sticks or straws into the playdough to make a porcupine.

Monkey, Monkey!

Too often parents focus on the bad things children do, while letting the good slip by without comment. This is a simple way to reinforce and reward cooperation and kindness.

Plastic linking monkeys

Hang a plastic monkey on the wall in a place where you can add more monkeys to make a chain. When you catch your child being especially kind and cooperative (that is, playing quietly with siblings, helping out without being asked, picking up toys without being reminded, and so on), reward her with a monkey to add to the chain. When the last monkey is hung, treat the whole family to an ice-cream sundae, video rental, or special afternoon of games.

Napkin Bug

Even much older children will have fun with this one.

Paper towel
Medium-size orange, grapefruit, or plastic ball
Pen or marker

Place the orange, grapefruit, or plastic ball on a flat surface
and put one piece of paper towel over it so that the fruit is
roughly centered under the towel. Cup your hand over the
paper towel so that it molds around the fruit (this is the body
of the bug). Using your other hand, twist each corner of the
paper towel until you have twisted right up to the body (these
are the legs). Use a pen or marker to draw a face on the bug,
then roll the fruit to make the bug run (the rather jerky roll
of the fruit gives the bug a funny little run). If you like, make
a couple of bugs and race them against each other.

I Think I Can

For this activity you'll need the book *The Little Engine That Could* by Watty Piper. A library will have a copy, but this is one of those books you'll want to own.

The Little Engine That Could

Read the book *The Little Engine That Could* to your child. Talk about how the little engine thought he could make it up the hill, even though it was a very hard thing to do. Ask your child if she thinks she can do something that may seem hard at first, then play the "I Think I Can" game. Ask your child to try different things like "Can you hop on one foot?" or "Can you touch your toes?" Demonstrate for her, then say "I think I can, I think I can" as you hop or bend together. Try this game when you're encouraging your child to pick up her toys. ("Do you think you can put away all your cars before I pick up these puzzles?")

Interrupt Rule

I wish I had come across this idea when my children were younger. Although they've always been polite interrupters, even "Excuse me, Mommy" repeated twenty times can be annoying. Worse still is the adult who breaks off midsentence to turn full attention to the interrupting child.

When you're talking on the phone or in person with someone, teach your child how to interrupt politely. Show her how to place her hand on your arm, shoulder, or leg. This will be her signal that she needs your attention. Place your hand over hers as your signal that you understand and will acknowledge her as soon as politely possible. Very young children should not be made to wait more than 10 or 15 seconds, but this time can and should grow longer as your child becomes used to this rule.

Mini Mask

Paper
Scissors
Pencil, markers, or crayons
25-cent coin

Cut a small (4- to 6-inch) square of paper. Place the coin in the middle of the square and trace around it. Draw eyes above the circle and a mouth below it. Be creative in adding eyelashes, eyebrows, or a funny mustache. Cut out the eyes and nose and put the mask on your child's face by placing the center hole over her nose.

Early Morning Fun

If your toddler is an early riser, you may find this idea will give you a few extra minutes of precious sleep.

Basket or small plastic crate
2–3 quiet toys, games, or activities

Before you go to bed at night, put two or three quiet toys, games, or activities in a basket or small plastic crate. Be sure that the items you choose are completely safe for your child to play with unsupervised. Place the basket or crate in your toddler's crib or beside her bed. The toys or activities may keep her occupied long enough for you to make the coffee, have a shower, or just enjoy a little extra sleep!

People Puppets

Photos of family members
Glue or tape
Clear contact paper
Popsicle sticks

Use glue or tape to attach a Popsicle stick to the back of a photograph. Cover with clear contact paper for an instant puppet.

Cartons of Fun

This idea is recommended for older two- and three-year-olds, as younger children will likely not get any more creative than dumping the contents on the floor.

Empty milk cartons or other containers
Miscellaneous craft items

Fill clean empty milk cartons with an assortment of craft items: scraps of fabric, ribbon, wrapping paper, bows, stickers, glue, safety scissors, and so on. Bring out the carton for a fun and creative playtime.

Cereal Box Puzzle

A colorful cereal box can make an inexpensive jigsaw puzzle tailored to your child's age and ability.

Empty cereal box
Scissors

Cut out the front panel of an empty cereal box. Cut into interlocking shapes, making the size of the pieces and the difficulty of the puzzle appropriate for the child who will be putting the puzzle together.

Easy Bird Feeder

Feeding the birds is fun, but once you start, it's important to keep it up for the whole season. Birds will come to rely on the food you provide and may have difficulty finding another food source if you suddenly stop.

Round oat cereal or circular pretzels
Heavy string, yarn, or a shoelace

String round oat cereal or circular pretzels onto heavy string, yarn, or a shoelace. Tie the ends together and hang in a tree to feed the birds.

People Blocks

Pictures of family members
Clear contact paper
Rectangular wood blocks or clean, empty food cans

Use clear contact paper to attach photographs of your family to rectangular blocks of wood or clean, empty food cans. Your child will love building structures with her people blocks.

Magic Mud

Kids of all ages love this one. Magic Mud feels like a solid, but it just drips through your fingers.

1 box cornstarch
Water
Food coloring

Put the cornstarch in a bowl. Add just enough water to be able to stir the mixture, then add food coloring. Your child may want to use her fingers to play with this, but it's great for running cars through, too.

Squishy Bag

3 cups water
4 tablespoons cornstarch
Food coloring
Ziploc bag

Boil the water. In a separate bowl, add cold water to the cornstarch to make a paste. Slowly add the cornstarch mixture to the boiled water. Cook and stir until thick. Add food coloring and allow to cool. Pour into a Ziploc bag and seal. Children can squish the bag without opening it.

Flying Fish

Your child will enjoy tossing these fish into the air and watching them gently flutter down.

Page from an old magazine
Pencil
Ruler
Scissors

Using the ruler, pencil, and scissors, mark and cut a strip of the magazine page that is as long as the page and 1 inch wide. Mark a line on each end of the strip that is 1 inch from the end. Cut a slit halfway into the strip at each point. (At one end of the strip cut from the top halfway down to the middle, and at the other end cut from the bottom halfway up to the middle.) Bend the strip into a loop and push the slits together so that the loop closes. Toss the fish into the air to see it fly.

No-Cook Squishy Bag

Try the following no-cook alternatives to the Squishy Bag. Make sure the bag is well-sealed before letting your child squish it. You can vary the sensory experience by warming or chilling the contents before giving the bag to your toddler. You could also use two bags at a time—one warm and one cold.

hair gel and a few drops of food coloring
ketchup and mustard
shaving cream with or without food coloring
toothpaste
hand lotion
thick fingerpaint
pudding
snow (for a temporary and seasonal activity)

Painting Bag

Although this idea uses paint, I think it's too neat and clean to include with the other painting activities. It's quick and fun for anytime—not just when you've got the time and energy for a painting project.

3 tablespoons powdered tempera paint
¼ cup liquid laundry starch (optional)
Ziploc bag
Construction paper

Mix the powdered tempera paint with liquid laundry starch. Pour it into the bag and smooth out the bubbles. If you don't have liquid laundry starch, just prepare the tempera paint fairly thick or use fingerpaint. Make sure the bag is well-sealed, then show your child how to press the bag to make designs. Place a piece of construction paper under the bag (use a different color than the paint) and notice how it seems to change the color of the paint.

Toddler Pouch

Toddlers love to collect things in their pockets. Your child will enjoy wearing this little pouch and using it to store all her interesting discoveries.

2 paper plates
Scissors
Stapler
Hole punch
Yarn or ribbon

Cut one paper plate in half. Staple one half to the second paper plate to form a pouch. Punch two holes in the top of the full paper plate, then tie a short length of yarn or ribbon from one hole to the next to form a handle. (Because of the danger of strangulation, please make sure that the yarn or ribbon is not long enough to go over your child's head.) Decorate it with crayons, markers, or stickers. Hang the pouch from your child's belt or let her carry it around with her.

Pipe Play

10- to 20-foot length of 1-inch PVC pipe
PVC joints

Cut a 10- to 20-foot length of 1-inch PVC pipe into various lengths ranging from 4 to 10 inches. Add various PVC joints to serve as connectors. (These come straight or in a T, L or + shape.) Your child should have years of fun building structures with these pipes and connectors.

In fine weather, your child will enjoy building things outside. Add a garden hose so she can run water through her pipes.

Tubes and Balls

Small balls such as golf balls, Ping-Pong balls, or tennis balls
*Cardboard tubes from empty paper towel rolls or large gift-
  wrap rolls*
Scissors
Box or basket

Collect a variety of small balls that are big enough to avoid a choking hazard. Cut various widths of cardboard tubes into different lengths. Put the balls and tubes in a box or basket and let your child have fun dropping the balls through the tubes.

Tube Fun

A short length of flexible transparent tubing from the hardware store can be used in several ways to provide some simple fun for your toddler.

3-foot length of flexible transparent tubing,
  about 1 inch in diameter
Marbles
Cork
Glue gun

Glue a cork securely in one end of the tube. Put several marbles inside the tube and glue a cork in the other end. Your child will have fun seeing the marbles roll as she lifts the tube by one end or in the middle. For an alternative, use a shorter length of tubing and fill with vegetable oil before adding the marbles. (Be sure the corks fit very tightly for this one!)

Tube Ball

Large cardboard mailing tube or gift-wrap tube
Tennis ball
String
Empty basket or box

Tie a large cardboard tube to a stair railing, making the end of
the tube even with the end of the railing. Place a basket or
box at the end of the tube. Your toddler will enjoy placing the
ball in one end and watching it shoot out the other end into
the basket. This will keep your little one busy for a long time,
especially if she has to climb down the steps to retrieve the
ball and back up to play again. If you don't want her climbing
the steps on her own, give her a small stool to step on to
reach the top end of the tube, or avoid stools and steps altogether by placing one end of the tube on a couch and the
other end on the floor.

Net Ball

This makes a big, light ball that's safe and easy for even the youngest child to use indoors or out.

Onion-bag netting
Cotton batting or cotton balls
Twist tie or elastic band

Stuff the onion-bag netting with as much cotton as possible. Knot the top of the bag with a twist tie or elastic band.

Fun with Balls

Muffin pan
Tennis, golf, or Ping-Pong balls
Small basket or plastic container with handle (optional)

Give your toddler several tennis, golf, or Ping-Pong balls (or an assortment of all three) and an empty muffin pan. She will have fun putting the balls in each compartment, dumping them out, gathering them up, and starting all over again. If you like, provide her with a small basket or plastic container into which she can put the balls as she picks them up.

Toddler Blocks

Even number of empty milk cartons (any size will do)
Tape
Colorful contact paper, fabric, construction paper,
  or wrapping paper

Choose two milk cartons the same size. Measure the base of
one carton, and mark a cutting line that same distance up the
side of the carton. Cut along the line. Cut the other carton in
the same way. You should now have two open-ended cubes.
Push one cube open-end-down into the other cube. Tape
around the cut edges.

The cubes you make can be covered in any way you like.
Use colorful contact paper, construction paper, fabric, or wrapping paper. You can also glue on photos of your child, her
friends and family, or pictures from magazines. If using construction paper, wrapping paper, photos, or pictures, cover
with clear contact paper to make the block more durable.

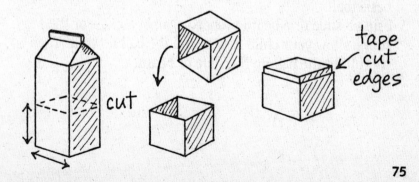

75

Balls, Balls, Balls

Children get so much enjoyment from balls. Instead of using a "real" ball, try using rolled-up socks, crumpled-up newsprint taped into a ball, or make a Net Ball (see page 74). These ideas can be easily adapted for either indoor or outdoor play.

Soft ball
Empty box or laundry basket
Slide or board

1. Sit opposite your child with your legs apart and take turns rolling the ball back and forth to each other.
2. Turn the box or basket on its side and show your child how to roll the ball into the target.
3. Place an empty box or laundry basket on the floor and have your child toss the ball into the basket from several feet away.
4. Place the basket on top of a dresser for a game of indoor basketball.
5. Using a slide or a board propped against a chair or the stairs, show your child how to roll the ball down it. Then try rolling the ball up the slide or board.

Sponge Blocks

Sponges make ideal blocks for toddlers. They are easy to hold, lightweight, and won't hurt anybody or anything if thrown.

Large, thick sponges

Purchase a colorful variety of large, thick sponges for your toddler to use as blocks. If you like, cut some in halves, quarters, triangular shapes, or other shapes. Store them in a laundry basket or plastic storage bin. Older toddlers may enjoy sorting sponges by color or making a pattern with them.

Stacking Fun

Individually wrapped toilet paper rolls
Small cans of tuna, tomato paste, and so on

Look around your house for interesting items for your toddler to stack. If you buy toilet paper in individually wrapped rolls, your child will have great fun using them to build towers. Small cans of tuna or tomato paste also stack nicely and are easy for little hands to manage.

Paper Bag Blocks

Toddlers love to lift and carry these big, light blocks. They're rather hard to store but easy to make again another day.

Paper grocery bags
Newspapers
Packing tape

Lay a paper bag flat on a floor or table. Fold the top over 6–8 inches and make a crease. Scrunch up newspaper one sheet at a time and fill the bag to the fold line. Fold the top over and tape the bag closed. If you like, paint or decorate the blocks before using. Make a tunnel for your child to crawl through or a tower for her to knock down, or just let her carry the blocks around the house.

Balloon Fun

Balloons
String
Plastic baseball bat, plastic golf club,
  gift-wrap tube, or rolled-up newsprint

Inflate five or six balloons and tie the ends securely. Attach a
length of string or ribbon to each balloon. Suspend the bunch
of balloons from the ceiling so that they hang just beyond
your child's reach. Let your toddler use a plastic baseball bat
or golf club to bat at the bunch of balloons. If you don't have
a bat or golf club, use a cardboard gift-wrap tube, or make a
bat by rolling up several sheets of newsprint and taping them
securely. Remember to supervise carefully when young children are playing with balloons.

Hide the Beanbag

Beanbag

Have your child close her eyes while you hide a beanbag within
a defined area. When she finds the beanbag, it's her turn to
hide it while you close your eyes.

More Balloon Fun

1 or more helium-filled balloons
String or ribbon

Attach a length of string or ribbon to a helium-filled balloon.
The string or ribbon should be just long enough so that your
child can reach the string when the balloon is resting on the
ceiling. Your child will have fun pulling the balloon down, letting it go, and watching it rise back up to the ceiling again.
Supervise carefully to avoid the danger of your child choking
on a piece of broken balloon.

Beanbag Throw

Beanbag
Basket

Throw a beanbag into a basket and ask your child to bring
you the beanbag. Repeat as long as this holds her attention.
She may want to try throwing the beanbag into the basket
herself or may just walk to the basket and drop it in.

Beanbag Crawl

Beanbag

Place a beanbag on your child's back while she's in a crawling position. Have her crawl around the room until the beanbag falls off. Two toddlers will enjoy playing this game, with one crawling and the other picking up the beanbag when it falls. Older children can play with a friend or sibling, seeing who can keep the beanbag on her back the longest.

Beanbag Races

One child can race against the clock, while two or more children can race against either the clock or each other.

Beanbag
Clock (optional)

Decide on a starting line and a finish line. Have children race with a beanbag balanced on their head or squeezed between their knees. For very young children, try balancing the beanbag in an open palm or kicking the beanbag across the finish line.

Indoor Baseball

Games such as this help your toddler develop eye-body coordination and are suitable for indoor as well as outdoor play.

Empty gift-wrap roll
Balloon

Play baseball with an inflated balloon and an empty gift-wrap roll. Take turns hitting, throwing, and running bases. Due to the extreme choking hazard posed by pieces of broken balloon, remember to always supervise carefully when young children are playing with balloons.

Toddler Bowling

Empty plastic soda bottles or unopened paper towel rolls
Large rubber ball

Line up three or four (or more) empty plastic soda bottles or unopened paper towel rolls. Show your toddler how to roll a large rubber ball to knock them over.

Balloon Play

Remember: Balloon pieces can pose an extreme choking hazard for children, so any balloon play with toddlers must be carefully supervised.

Wooden paint stirrer
Large paper plate
Glue gun
Balloons

Use a glue gun to attach a large paper plate to the end of a wooden paint stirrer. Throw the balloon up in the air and ask your toddler to try to catch the balloon in the paper plate, or have fun simply batting the balloon around. Put on some lively music to add to the fun.

Toddler Obstacle Course

An obstacle course is great fun for a group of toddlers at a birthday party, Sunday school class, playgroup, or other group setting. You can also use it at home for your own toddler or preschooler.

Come up with fun ideas for an obstacle course for your child or group. Bear in mind the ages, abilities, and number of children who will be involved, as well as the space you have available. Keep it simple to start with, and change the components of the course as they are mastered. Keep in mind that a toddler will need the help of an older child or adult to make it through the obstacle course, especially the first time.

The following ideas will get you started. Four or five stations are probably enough for a very young group. (Older preschoolers should be able to manage up to ten.)

- Jump over a rope.
- Walk along a balance board or a line of tape on the floor.
- Build a tower with blocks or other stackable objects.
- Roll a ball into a target or down a slide.
- Clip clothespins around the rim of a coffee can.
- String some beads on a shoelace.
- Draw a picture or scribble on a piece of paper.

- Play a game of newspaper golf with a rolled-up newspaper and a golf ball.
- Drop objects into a simple shape sorter.
- Play a simple matching game (correctly match up two sets of objects).
- Knock down paper towel rolls or empty soda bottles with a large ball.
- Thread canning rings on a wooden spoon.
- Crawl among or walk over chairs placed in a maze around the room.
- Jump into and out of a Hula-Hoop two or more times.

Mini Olympics

Paper plates and/or straws
Newspaper
Marker

Make a bull's-eye by drawing a large circle on a sheet of newspaper. Standing back a few feet, have your child try to throw a "discus" (paper plate) so that it lands on the bull's-eye. Vary this game by using drinking straws as javelins.

Big Mouth Game

Cardboard box
Markers
Scissors
Newspaper or tissue paper for decorating
Glue
Tennis balls or a rolled-up pair of socks

Draw a happy face on the side of a closed cardboard box. Make sure to draw a big, smiling, open mouth. Cut out the mouth. Add hair to the top of the box by gluing strips of newspaper or tissue paper so they hang down the sides. Stand back a suitable distance and see how many balls can be thrown into the mouth.

Musical Animals

This is an easier and more suitable (for younger children) version of the familiar musical chairs game.

1 stuffed animal for each player
1 chair for each player (optional)
Music

Place several chairs in a circle and put a stuffed animal on each chair, or place the animals in a circle on the floor. Toddlers walk around the circle and, when the music stops, each player picks up an animal and sits down. Players then take turns acting out that animal. If you don't have enough stuffed animals, paste pictures of various animals on sheets of paper and tape them to the chairs or place them in a circle on the floor.

If only you and your child are playing this game, try placing the stuffed animals inside a pillowcase. Then take turns removing an animal from the pillowcase and acting it out.

Unwrapping Game

Small toy
Wrapping paper
Tape

Wrap a small toy in wrapping paper. Show the wrapped toy to your toddler and ask, "What do you think is inside?" Give the wrapped toy to your child so she can remove the paper. Then rewrap the toy as your child watches. Let her unwrap it again, and repeat the game until she tires of it.

Flashlight Fun

Flashlight

Shine a flashlight on different parts of a room: a wall, the door, the floor, and so on. Each time you shine the light on an object, name it: for example, "This is the bed." Show your child how to turn the flashlight on and off. Let her shine it on various objects and name them. Give her directions to follow, such as "Shine the light on the ceiling."

CHAPTER 3
Kids in the Kitchen

"Children are natural mimics—they act like their parents in spite of every attempt to teach them good manners."
—*Anonymous*

Several times throughout this book you will read that for toddlers, it's the process—not the product—that counts. The value of an activity comes from what they do and what they learn rather than what they produce. That's certainly worth remembering for most activities, such as art and crafts, but in the kitchen it's a rather different story. In the kitchen the product does count! Kids may have fun dumping in a whole box of salt, and they may learn that salt comes quickly from the box when you turn it upside down, but unfortunately you will end up with an inedible product and a disappointed child!

A one-year-old will often be happy to sit in his highchair or at his own table with a small container of cereal or raisins to occupy him while you work. An empty egg carton to put his little snacks in will often keep him busy for a long time. But if he insists on helping, there are lots of ways to accommodate him without putting your delicious food in danger:

- Bake cupcakes and mix frosting ahead of time, and let your toddler frost the cupcakes with a small plastic knife or Popsicle stick.
- When making cookies, roll a bit of dough into a log and let your child use a plastic knife or Popsicle stick to cut the log into small pieces.
- Let your child pour premeasured ingredients and stir whenever possible.
- Give your child lettuce to tear for a salad and dressing to shake in a tightly closed plastic container.

The kitchen can be a great learning environment for your toddler, but the many irresistible things to see, touch, taste, and smell also make it a hazardous place for unsupervised children. Always be safety conscious. Make sure any dangerous objects are well out of reach, and closely supervise any use of sharp utensils, the oven, or the stove. Better yet, make a rule that only an adult can use those things.

The activities in this chapter suggest fun ways for toddlers to become involved in the preparation of food.

Letter Sandwiches

Alphabet cereal
Sliced wheat bread
Peanut butter, jam, or honey

Spread a few slices of bread with peanut butter, jam, or honey. Help your older toddler spell his name or a simple sentence such as "I love you" by applying the appropriate alphabet letters to his slice of bread. Younger toddlers will probably enjoy simply sticking the letters onto the bread in no particular order.

Pudding Paints

Packaged pudding mix

Prepare packaged pudding mix ahead of time and, when cooled, allow your child to fingerpaint on a tabletop, high-chair tray, plastic or paper plate, or other smooth surface. This activity may not be suitable before a meal, since there probably won't be much left to clean up!

Homemade Butter

Heavy cream
Baby-food jar or other small jar with a tight-fitting lid
Sieve or cheesecloth

Place the cream in the jar and cover it tightly with a lid. Your child can shake and shake and shake the jar until the cream forms soft lumps. Drain the lumpy cream through a sieve or cheesecloth and discard the liquid. Mash the remaining lumps in a bowl until they're smooth. Serve on muffins, bread, or crackers for a tasty snack.

Fruit Dips

Long plastic straws
Fruit cut into chunks
Yogurt (optional)

Cut a variety of fruits into chunks. These could include orange cubes, pineapple pieces, apple squares, strawberry bites, peach parts, whole grapes (or halves for very young children), and banana chunks. Show your child how to slide the pieces onto a long plastic straw. Eat them as is or dip them into yogurt for a great tasting, fun-to-eat snack.

Jell-O Paints

2–3 different colors of Jell-O

Prepare two or three different colors of Jell-O ahead of time. When set, place globs of each color on a tabletop, highchair tray, plastic or paper plate, or other smooth surface. Your child will have fun mucking about with this tasty fingerpaint, and eating it will not harm him!

Butterfly Sandwich

Bread
Cream cheese, peanut butter, or other bread spread
Bananas, raisins, pickles, and vegetable slices

Create an open-faced butterfly sandwich by cutting a slice of bread diagonally, then reversing the halves to form a butterfly. Spread with cream cheese, peanut butter, or other bread spread, then decorate with pickles, banana slices, raisins, or other pieces of soft fruit. Cut carrots or peppers in thin strips for antennae.

Picture Menus

If you like to give your child a choice at mealtime, but he tends to want the same meals day after day, picture menus may be the answer.

Pictures of your child's favorite meals
Heavy paper
Glue
Magnetic clip

Plan several different meals that you know your child likes, being sure to include a variety of healthy foods (fruits or vegetables, protein foods, and grains) in each one. Cut out pictures of each meal from grocery store flyers, coupons, product labels, or magazine pictures. Glue the pictures to index cards or pieces of heavy paper (one meal per page) and hang them on a magnetic clip on the refrigerator. After your child chooses a meal he'd like, move that card to a different location until all the cards have been used up, then start over. Your child still has a choice, but there will be less arguing, indecision, and monotony.

What Is It?

Scarf for blindfolding
Various objects to touch, smell, and taste

Challenge your child's senses by blindfolding him and giving him objects to identify using his sense of touch, smell, and taste. Very young children (or children who object to being blindfolded) can simply close their eyes. Start with something easy such as a banana or cracker. Try nonfood items as well (a feather or a favorite toy), and be prepared to take a turn at the challenge yourself.

Vegetable Teethers

Frozen mixed vegetables

Serve your teething toddlers frozen mixed vegetables straight from the freezer. Most kids like them better uncooked, and they can be a quick fix for those fussy times.

Apple Smile

Red apple (unpeeled)
Peanut butter
Miniature marshmallows

Cut a crisp apple into wedges. When laid on its side, each wedge should look like a lip. Spread one side of an apple wedge with peanut butter. Add three or four miniature marshmallow "teeth" along the edge. Spread another apple wedge with peanut butter. Place it on top of the marshmallows for a big, toothy grin.

No-Bake Banana Cookies

Graham crackers
Rolling pin
Ziploc bag
Banana or other fruit

Place three graham crackers in a Ziploc bag and crush them with a rolling pin. Slice a banana or other fruit into small pieces. Shake a few pieces at a time into the bag to completely coat the fruit. Lay the pieces out on a plate and, if you like, provide a little fork for spearing.

Fruit Popsicles

Baby food (or puréed fruit)
Unsweetened fruit juice

Empty a jar of baby food into a measuring cup. Add unsweetened fruit juice to make 1 cup. Stir well and pour into a four-section Popsicle mold. Insert handles and freeze until set. To double the recipe, add another cup of juice.

Bananas, Honey, and Wheat Germ

This is a sticky activity but a banana lover's delight!

Banana
Honey
Milk
Wheat germ
Plastic knives or Popsicle sticks

Mix some honey with a little milk to thin it, then put it in a small bowl. Put some wheat germ in a second small bowl. Cut a banana in half and give your child a half to peel. Let him cut his banana half into smaller pieces with a plastic knife or Popsicle stick. Show him how to dip a banana chunk first into the honey bowl, then into the wheat germ. He may want to eat it right away, or you can place each dipped chunk on a small plate to save for later.

Ants on a Log

This easy, no-bake treat is fun to make and healthy, too!

Celery stalks
Small plastic knife or Popsicle stick
Peanut butter
Raisins

Wash and cut celery stalks into 3- or 4-inch sticks. Give your child a small plastic knife or a Popsicle stick and show him how to spread peanut butter onto the celery. Stick raisins in the peanut butter and eat.

If your child has an allergy to peanut butter, use cheese spread, cream cheese, jam, or honey.

Peanut Butter Sculptures

I don't know which part of this activity children enjoy more: building the sculpture or eating it!

Peanut butter
Crackers
Small plastic knife or Popsicle stick

Put peanut butter on a small plate or in a small plastic container (unless you don't mind your toddler sticking his fingers into the whole jar). If your child has an allergy to peanut butter, use cheese spread, cream cheese, jam, or honey. Show your child how to spread the peanut butter onto a cracker, then stick another cracker on top of it. Use a few different kinds of crackers if possible. Even animal crackers are fun.

Washing Vegetables

Small basin of water
Vegetable brush or dishcloth
Vegetables or fruit to wash
Dishtowel for drying

Fill a small basin with several inches of water. Give your child several pieces of fruit or vegetables to wash in the basin. He may enjoy using a vegetable brush or gently rubbing them with a dishcloth. When they are clean, show him how to dry the fruit or vegetables with a clean dishtowel.

Mud Balls

1 cup peanut butter
¼ cup honey
½ cup dry powdered milk
½ cup raisins
Crushed graham crackers
Chocolate milk powder

Mix all ingredients together in a medium-size bowl. Show your toddler how to form the mixture into balls. Place a small amount of chocolate milk powder on a plate and roll the balls in the powder. Eat as a tasty snack or refrigerate and serve later.

Dump Cake

This is the type of cake about which even a very young child can boast, "I made it all by myself."

20-ounce can crushed pineapple
16-ounce can cherry pie filling
Yellow cake mix
¾ cup butter or margarine

Butter a 9-inch by 13-inch baking pan. Dump in the crushed pineapple, including the juice, and spread evenly. Spoon the cherry pie filling evenly over the pineapple. Sprinkle the yellow cake mix over the fruit. Slice the butter or margarine thinly and place the pieces on top of the cake mix. Bake at 350°F for 45 minutes.

Fruit Salad

Younger toddlers can help cut the bananas and perhaps the canned fruit with a plastic knife. They can also dump and mix the ingredients. Older toddlers can do most of the cutting with a dull knife. This recipe makes enough salad for a group of toddlers, so adjust the quantities as needed.

Canned peaches
Canned pears
Canned pineapple
Bananas
Apples
Vanilla yogurt

Open the canned fruit and cut pieces small enough for toddlers to eat. Peel and slice bananas and apples. Mix it all in a large bowl with vanilla yogurt and serve to toddlers in small bowls.

Painted Toast

2 tablespoons milk
Food coloring
Clean paintbrush
White bread
Toaster

Mix the milk with a few drops of food coloring in a small container. Use a paintbrush to paint designs or faces on the bread. Then toast the bread, butter it, and eat it, or use it to make a sandwich.

Marshmallow Treats

These treats aren't very nutritious, but toddlers will love to help make their own colorful snack.

Regular-size marshmallows
Jell-O powder
Ziploc bag

Pour some Jell-O powder into a Ziploc bag. Insert a marshmallow or two, seal the bag, and shake. Remove the coated marshmallows from the bag and eat.

Apple Shake-Ups

Apple
Knife
Sugar
Cinnamon
Ziploc bag

Peel an apple and cut it into toddler-size pieces. Or cut it into larger slices and have your older toddler use a plastic knife to cut it into smaller pieces. Place 1–2 tablespoons of sugar and about ½ teaspoon of cinnamon into a Ziploc bag. Add a few apple pieces, seal the bag, and shake to coat the apples. Remove the coated apples from the bag and eat.

Zoo Sandwiches

Sliced bread
Cream cheese
Cream
Food coloring (optional)
Plastic knives
Animal cookie cutters

Combine cream cheese with cream in a mixing bowl (1 table-spoon of cream per 3 ounces of cream cheese). Mix with a spoon until the cream cheese is soft. Add a few drops of food coloring, if desired, and stir well. Cut bread in animal shapes with the cookie cutters. Use a small plastic knife or Popsicle stick to spread the cream cheese mixture on the bread.

If your child is not fond of cream cheese, use peanut butter, honey, or jam instead.

Quickie Cookies

These cookies aren't very nutritious either, but older toddlers can practically make them on their own. There's no measuring if you use premeasured margarine squares, and cleanup is a breeze with only a bowl, mixing spoon, and cookie sheets.

1 package cake mix
½ cup butter or margarine
1 egg

Mix all the ingredients in a medium-size bowl. Mold into balls and place on greased cookie sheets. Bake at 350°F for about 10 minutes or until done. Cool for a few minutes on the cookie sheet, then remove to a cooling rack to cool completely.

Pudding Cookies

1 cup Bisquick baking mix
1 small package instant pudding
¼ cup vegetable oil
1 egg
⅓ cup peanut butter (optional)
Chocolate chips, raisins, coconut (optional)
White sugar
Cinnamon candies or chocolate chips
  for decorating (optional)

Combine Bisquik, instant pudding, oil, and egg in a bowl. Mix in peanut butter, chocolate chips, raisins, or coconut if desired. Roll the dough into balls and put them on an ungreased cookie sheet. Dip the bottom of a glass in sugar and press it on each ball until flattened. If making plain dough, cookies may be decorated with red cinnamon candies or chocolate chips before baking. Bake at 350°F for 8 minutes. Makes two to three dozen cookies.

CHAPTER 4

Water Play

"A lot of people assume that because I am the mother of ten children, I must be an expert on motherhood, but such is not the case. It is true that I have learned a great deal over the years, but fortunately I have managed to forget most of what I have learned. (That is how I have remained sane.)"
—*Teresa Bloomingdale*

For young children, water isn't just for getting clean. In fact, water play for toddlers is rarely about getting clean. Dumping, pouring, filling, mixing, playing with sponges, corks, cups, bowls, soap, ice cubes, and so on is a lot of fun for toddlers and preschoolers. It also encourages discovery and stimulates interest in the physical world.

Water play can also help parents and other caregivers maintain their sanity. During the early months of my third pregnancy, my two-year-old and one-year-old played happily in the bath on many rainy mornings. It was a great way for them to have fun while I did as little as possible!

Most toddlers probably have at least one water-play session per day: bathtime. Here are a few suggestions to help your child get the maximum amount of fun out of every bath:

- Put a few inches of water in the tub, place your child in the water, then let the tap run slowly so your child can fill up cups, play in the stream of water, and so on.
- Add as many plastic kitchen utensils as you can spare to your collection of bath toys.
- Sponges (plain or cut into shapes) are fun for the bath.
- Toddlers will love filling up small containers with water.
- Add inflated balloons, corks, or ice cubes to the bath. (Supervise carefully to prevent choking on small items or bits of broken balloon.)
- A Ping-Pong ball is lots of fun in the tub. Try to keep it under the water—it will always pop up!
- Poke a few holes in the bottom of a plastic container. Children will enjoy filling it with water and watching the water drip and dribble out the bottom.
- Make up a batch of Bubble Solution (see page 135) and blow bubbles as your child has her bath.

If your toddler is like mine, she loves to line up her little cups and other containers along the edge of the bathtub and then repeatedly fill them up, dump them out, and fill them up again. While great fun for children, this activity usually results in a lot of water on the bathroom floor (and, in some cases, a lot of water leaking through to the ceiling of the room below). A small, Rubbermaid-type step stool placed in the bathtub gives your child a great platform for her containers and helps keep most of the water in the tub.

Water play is also a great kitchen activity. Most toddlers will enjoy standing on a chair at the kitchen sink and playing in a sinkful of water with bowls, cups, and other containers. If you have a dishwasher in your kitchen, the open door of a clean, empty dishwasher makes a great water play table for your toddler. Simply add a bucket of water and some small cups and containers to fill and dump. A thick towel in front of the sink or under the open dishwasher door will help soak up spills.

The following ideas for water play cover a variety of situations—both indoors and out. You may find some of these ideas better suited to older toddlers and preschoolers. Remember: Drowning in a water-filled bucket or a few inches of water in the bathtub is a very real possibility for toddlers, so please supervise any water play carefully.

Wash the Floor

Sponge

Give your child a wet sponge and let her help you when you're washing the floor. Once you know she will not automatically dump it, give her an inch or two of water in a small bucket or bowl. She will have fun being your helper, and cleanup is easy!

Cork Race

You will need one of each of the following items for each player. Many toddlers haven't yet mastered the skill of blowing through a straw, so you may want to save this idea for when your child is a little older.

Cork
9-inch by 13-inch baking pans
Straw

Fill each baking pan with water and place the pans on a table or on the floor. Give each player a cork and a straw. The winner is the first one to blow her cork from one side of the pan to the other.

Fun with Water

If you don't mind water all over the floor, you can use this idea inside. Otherwise, you may want to save it for a warm day outdoors. Young toddlers tend to have more fun dumping the bucket rather than playing with the dishes and utensils, so try using a bucket that, when filled, is too heavy for a toddler to lift. (A large, clean, empty laundry- or dishwasher-detergent container works well.)

Large plastic basin or bucket
Various kitchen utensils: spoons, eggbeater, whisk, and so on
Plastic bowls and dishes
Small plastic bottles
Funnel

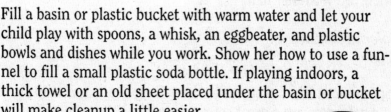

Fill a basin or plastic bucket with warm water and let your child play with spoons, a whisk, an eggbeater, and plastic bowls and dishes while you work. Show her how to use a funnel to fill a small plastic soda bottle. If playing indoors, a thick towel or an old sheet placed under the basin or bucket will make cleanup a little easier.

Waterfall Game

Pennies
Bowl, cup, or other container
Water

Fill a container almost to the top with water. Give each player a supply of pennies. Take turns dropping a penny into the container. The game ends when one player drops in the penny that makes the water overflow.

Michelangelo's Bathroom

Try this idea if your child hates getting water on her face when you wash her hair.

Colorful pictures
Tape

Tape some colorful pictures to the ceiling over your bathtub. (Old calendars are a great source for these.) Your child can look at the pictures and talk with you about them as you wash her hair. Unless she has a favorite, change the pictures often to maintain interest.

Soap Crayons

These are fun to write with in the tub or to use when washing little hands.

1½ cup pure soap powder (Ivory Snow)
Food coloring
½ cup water
Small containers or ice cube tray

Mix water and soap powder together. Add enough food coloring to get the color you want. If you'd like more than one color, divide the mixure into two or three small containers before adding food coloring. Pour the colored soap into a small container (empty plastic film canisters work well) or an ice cube tray, or mold it into crayon shapes and let harden before using.

Water Balloon Catch

Balloons
Water

Fill several balloons with water and play catch with them, or use sidewalk chalk to draw a target on the sidewalk and aim for that instead.

Drown the Penny

Paper towel
Glass filled with water
Pencil
Rubber band
Penny

Place the paper towel over the water-filled glass. Wrap a rubber band around the top of the glass to hold the paper towel in place. Place the penny on the paper towel in the center of the glass. Take turns poking holes in the paper towel with the pencil. The game ends when someone drowns the penny by poking the hole that finally makes the penny sink to the bottom of the glass.

Bathtub Soap Paint

You may want to skip this idea if your child has sensitive skin.

½ cup pure soap flakes (Ivory Snow)
¾ cup water
Food coloring
Electric mixer or wire whisk
Paintbrush
Spray bottle

Use an electric mixer or wire whisk to whip the soap flakes and water together until you get the texture of shaving cream. Add food coloring (be careful—it can stain the grout around ceramic tiles and should be omitted if this worries you). Use a brush to paint the wall around the bathtub. Give your child a spray bottle filled with water and let her spray the paint off.

Water Play

This bathtime variation is great for long, rainy days.

Plastic baby bathtub
Bath toys

Sit your diapered child in an empty bathtub. Fill a plastic baby bathtub or other large container with water and set it beside your child. Provide an assortment of bath toys that she can play with. (Cups, spoons, bowls, funnels, empty squeeze bottles, a plastic teapot, and sponges all make excellent water play toys.)

Bathtime Bubbles

Bubble solution
Bubble blower

Blow bubbles for your child while she sits in the bath. Have her try to catch them in her open hands or clap her hands together to pop them.

Colored Ice Cubes

Ice cubes will melt fairly quickly in a warm bath, but they can still be a choking hazard for little ones. Please supervise carefully.

Ice cube tray
Water
Food coloring

Make colored ice cubes by adding a drop of food coloring to the water in each section of an ice cube tray. Freeze. Add a bowl of different-colored ice cubes to the bath for some bathtime fun.

Sponge Play

Sponges
Water
2 bowls or other containers

Fill one bowl with water and add a few drops of food coloring if you like. Show your toddler how to place the sponge in the bowl of water, then transfer the water to the empty bowl by squeezing the sponge.

Ice Blocks

If small ice cubes melt too quickly, try making a larger block of ice to play with in the bath or outside on a warm summer day.

Clean milk carton
Water
Food coloring (optional)
Small plastic toys (optional)

Make an ice block by freezing water in a clean milk carton. If you like, add a few drops of food coloring to the water before freezing, or drop in a few small plastic toys. Your child will enjoy playing with the block in the bath or outside in the pool. If you've frozen small plastic toys inside the block, watch your child's surprise as the ice melts and the toys appear.

As a variation, fill balloons with water, tie tightly, and freeze to make ice balls.

Toddler Sprinkler

This idea may become a real hit around your house—outside, of course!

Large plastic bottle (gallon milk jugs work great)
Hammer and nail

Use a hammer and nail to poke holes in the bottom of a large plastic bottle. When you're outside, fill the bottle with water and let your child sprinkle the grass, flowers, sidewalk, driveway, and so on.

Baster Play

In *The Preschooler's Busy Book,* I suggest this activity using an eyedropper. Toddlers will enjoy doing the same with a large baster.

Kitchen baster
Plastic bowls or other containers
Water

Fill one bowl with water and add a few drops of food coloring if you like. Show your toddler how to place the baster in the bowl full of water and squeeze the bulb. She will enjoy watching the tube fill up with water. Show her how to hold the baster over an empty container and let go of the bulb to release the water.

Rock Drop

Wading pool, large bucket, or dishpan
Water
Rocks large enough to pass the choke test

Put a few inches of water in a wading pool, large bucket, or dishpan and let your toddler drop the rocks into the water.

Water Rhythms

A toddler with a hose will have a good time, no doubt about it. Upside-down pots add a dimension of sound for some extra fun.

Metal pots and lids
Garden hose with spray attachment

Turn the pots upside down on the grass or driveway. Prop up some of the pot lids against a wall or fence. Turn on the water and let your toddler spray the pots and lids to hear the drumming noises.

Ball Splash

Wading pool
Water
Large beach ball

Fill a wading pool with a few inches of water. Face your toddler across the pool and take turns throwing a beach ball hard at the water, trying to splash each other and yourself.

Target Practice

This is a great game for a summer get-together or birthday party. If your child isn't old enough to shoot a squirt gun, try using the garden hose instead.

32-ounce plastic soda bottles
Ping-Pong balls
Squirt gun or garden hose

Fill three or four plastic soda bottles with water. Set the bottles on a level surface. (A child's picnic table works well.) Place a Ping-Pong ball on top of each bottle. Use the squirt gun or garden hose to try to shoot the balls off the bottles.

Ice Play

This is a great outdoor idea for a hot day. If you'd rather do this inside, sit your toddler in an empty bathtub with the pan of ice beside her.

Crushed ice
Plastic dishpan or large bowl
Bath toys

Put some crushed ice into a plastic dishpan or large plastic bowl. Your child will have fun using her bath toys (cups, spoons, bowls, and so on) to play with the ice. If you're making the ice instead of buying it, add a few drops of food coloring to the water before freezing it.

Sponge Tag

Sponges
Bucket of water

Soak sponges in water, then have fun throwing them at each other. If your child doesn't like the idea of being the target, try throwing sponges at a tree or garage door, or use sidewalk chalk to draw a big circle or other shapes and aim for that instead.

Colored Sand

Spray bottle
Water
Food coloring or liquid paint

Fill a spray bottle with water and add a few drops of food coloring or a few spoonfuls of liquid paint. Let your child spray the sand in the sandbox to make a colorful desert. Turn the sand over with a shovel and watch the color disappear. Now your child can start all over again.

Car Wash

Bucket of warm, soapy water
Cloth or sponge
Hose
Riding toys

Help your child set up a toddler car wash. Give her a bucket of warm, soapy water and a cloth or sponge, and let her wash her riding toys. She may need help using the hose to rinse them when she's finished.

Gone Fishing

Large bucket or dishpan
Water
Plastic worm lures (without hooks)
Scoop or small strainer (optional)
Corks, Ping-Pong balls, or small sponge scraps (optional)

Fill a large bucket or dishpan with water. Add a few plastic worm lures and let your toddler have fun trying to catch them in her hands or in a scoop or small strainer. For variety, float corks, Ping-Pong balls, or small sponge scraps in the water. Encourage your toddler to scoop them out one by one.

Wet the Chalkboard

Chalkboard
Sponge or large paint brush
Water

Encourage your child to paint or wipe the chalkboard with a wet sponge or large paintbrush dipped in water. She will enjoy seeing it darken as it gets wet.

Funnels and Tubes

*12- to 18-inch length of flexible plastic tubing, ½ inch in
    diameter*
Funnel
Plastic measuring cup or small container
Dishpan or large bucket
Food coloring

Fill the dishpan or large bucket with water. Add a few drops of
food coloring to make colored water. Attach a funnel to one end
of the flexible plastic tubing. (If it doesn't stay securely, you
may want to use a glue gun to permanently join the two.) Place
the other end of the tubing in the dishpan or bucket. Show
your toddler how to scoop up some water from the bucket and
pour it into the funnel. She will enjoy watching the colored
water flow through the tubing and back into the bucket. If you
like, use two buckets and have her transfer water from one
bucket to another with her cup, funnel, and tubing.

CHAPTER 5

Outdoor Adventures

"As soon as I stepped out of my mother's womb on to dry land, I realized that I had made a mistake, that I shouldn't have come, but the trouble with children is that they are not returnable."
—*Quentin Crisp*

Outdoor play every day, in almost any weather, is essential for children of all ages. Whether playing in the snow, picking spring flowers, crunching fall leaves, or stomping in puddles after a rain, toddlers need to be outdoors to master their new-found skills of walking, running, climbing, and jumping.

Whatever the weather, toddlers will almost certainly find something with which to amuse themselves. Most never tire of sand and water play, and swings and slides are a great deal of fun as well as a great way to work off some of their seem-ingly endless energy. Whether you push a stroller, pull a wagon, or walk with your child at a toddler's pace, both par-ent and child will benefit from short walks outdoors almost every day.

The ideas in this chapter will provide some fun and inter-esting things to do with your toddler outdoors. Most require a minimum of materials, and you will find that with minor changes, most are suitable for any season and any weather. Many indoor-play ideas in Chapter 2 and water-play ideas in Chapter 4 are also easily adaptable to outdoor play.

Measuring Magic

Measuring cups and spoons
Bowls or small containers
Water, sand, or mud

Give your child an assortment of cups, spoons, bowls, and other containers and let him play outdoors with water, sand, or mud.

Spaghetti Splash

We tried this in our backyard one warm summer day as part of our playgroup wind-up. After many years have passed, my children and the parents who attended still talk about it! Watch out, though, it can kill the grass!

2–3 packages cooked spaghetti
⅓ cup vegetable oil
Food coloring
Child's wading pool

Mix the ingredients in a child's wading pool. Children may want to play with the spaghetti with their hands, sit in it, or (as we tried) use a small slide to get right into the middle of it.

Mud Handprints

Mud
Sturdy paper or plastic plate
Spatula or knife for smoothing

Fill the plate with thick mud and smooth into a flat, even surface. Have your child press his open hand into the mud and remove. Place the mud in the sun to dry. This won't last, but it's fun to look at for a while. For lasting prints, use plaster of Paris.

Bubble Solutions

The following three bubble-solution recipes come from
Science World in Vancouver, British Columbia. They say the
following about glycerine: "Not all detergents require the
addition of glycerine in order to make good soap solutions.
Glycerine helps soap bubbles hold water and this helps to
keep the bubbles from popping. Try a tablespoon or two for a
small batch (we're not exact about it). Glycerine can be purchased at most pharmacies. You won't need much, so don't go
buying caseloads."

All-Purpose Bubble Solution

Here's a good all-purpose solution for most bubble tricks,
experiments, and activities.

7–10 parts water
1 part dish detergent
Glycerine

Combine water, detergent, and 1–2 tablespoons of glycerine
(see note above) in a bowl or plastic container.

Thick Bubble Solution

This is a thick, goopy solution that forms bubbles strong enough to withstand a small puff of air. You can blow bubbles inside of bubbles with this mixture, and you don't need a straw. Just make a bubble and blow!

2½–3 parts water
1 part dish detergent
Glycerine

Combine water, detergent, and 1–2 tablespoons of glycerine (see note above) in a bowl or plastic container.

Bouncy Bubble Solution

This is a fun solution that you can bounce off your clothes.

2 packages unflavored gelatin
4 cups hot water (just boiled)
3–5 tablespoons glycerine
3 tablespoons dish detergent

Dissolve the gelatin in hot water. Add glycerine and dish detergent. This mixture will gel, so you'll need to reheat it whenever you use it.

Bubble Fun

Plastic drinking straws
Store-bought or homemade bubble solution (see Bubble
  Solutions on page 135)
Scissors
Tape

Make a bubble wand by cutting two plastic drinking straws in half, then taping the four pieces together. Blowing through the straws will send lots of tiny bubbles in many directions.

Jell-O Jumping

4 large packages Jell-O
Baby bathtub

Prepare Jell-O according to package directions. Place it in a baby's bathtub or small basin and let your child stand in it, sit in it, run his fingers through it, or paint with it.

Frog in the Grass

4 green rubber frogs (or rubber snakes,
  beanbags, or small plastic toys)

Have your child stand on the far side of the yard and close his eyes. Hide the frogs in the grass in different spots around the yard. When you yell "Frog in the grass!" your child must run and find the frogs. Make sure he grabs them before they hop away!

Red, Red, Red

You can play this game with a group of children or when it's just you and your child.

Have the players stand next to each other behind a starting line. The leader calls out three colors (for example, "Red, red, red!"). If the colors don't match ("Red, red, yellow!"), no one moves. If the colors do match, then children run, skip, or hop to a distant point and back. Feel free to substitute animals ("Cat, cat, dog!"), body parts ("Hand, hand, foot!"), or whatever you like.

Leaf Scrunch

Dry leaves
Small box
Contact paper

Collect dry leaves in a bag on an autumn walk with your child. At home, dump the leaves into a box and let your child scrunch the leaves with his hands. Use some of the colorful pieces to make a fall collage on a piece of clear contact paper.

Balloon Kites

Flying a kite is difficult and frustrating for toddlers and preschoolers. These "kites" are guaranteed to fly, even on days with light wind.

Large, round helium balloons
Kite string
Paper streamers (optional)

Tie one end of a long length of kite string to a round helium balloon and the other to your child's wrist. He will find it fun and easy to fly his balloon, and you won't worry about crashes and tangles. Try attaching lengths of paper streamers to the balloon to give it a more authentic kite look.

Dodge Ball

This is a fun game for four or more children.

Large, soft ball (try crumpled up newspaper and tape, or onion-bag netting stuffed with cotton balls or batting)

Have children form a circle with one child in the middle. Each player in the outer circle takes a turn throwing the ball at the child in the middle, who tries to dodge out of the way. When the child in the middle gets hit, he changes places with the child who hit him.

Toddler Ball

Plastic ball
Plastic bat and tee (optional)

Show your child how to throw or kick a plastic ball, or have him try hitting it with a plastic bat off a tee. Pick up the ball and chase your child to a "base" (a tree or other designated point) and then back to "home." You may want to tag your child occasionally, but let him be "safe" sometimes, too.

Shadow Tracing

Chalk

Go outside with your child on a sunny day. If your child will stand still long enough, trace his shadow on the sidewalk or driveway. Have him change positions, then trace his shadow again. Make several tracings, then see if your child can fit his shadow back inside the tracings.

For a fun alternative, trace his shadow on a big sheet of newsprint or other paper. Let him fingerpaint his shadow or color it with crayons or markers.

Digging for Treasure

Small objects to hide
Shovels
Colander
Sandbox

Hide small objects in the sandbox for your toddler to find as he digs about. Try using an old kitchen colander to sift through the sand. If you like, spray-paint rocks in shiny silver and gold, and show your toddler how to search for hidden treasure.

Nature Bracelet

Masking tape
Scissors

Before going outdoors with your child, wrap a piece of masking tape to his wrist, sticky side up. As you explore, help him attach colorful leaves, flowers, and other interesting discoveries to his bracelet. When done, use scissors to snip off the nature bracelet. Display on a bulletin board, shelf, or wall.

Changing Colors

This is a good activity for outdoors or in, and will also entertain children on a long car ride.

Colored cellophane in various colors

Give your child a piece of colored cellophane. Go for a walk outside and encourage your child to look at familiar objects through the cellophane. Your child will enjoy seeing how the color of everyday objects changes when seen through the cellophane. If you like, change the color of cellophane your child is using, or look through two pieces of cellophane at once to see how the colors change yet again.

Snow Painting

You'll have the prettiest yard in the neighborhood after this activity!

Spray bottle
Water
Food coloring or liquid tempera paint

Fill a spray bottle with water and add a few drops of food coloring or a spoon or two of liquid tempera paint. Dress your child warmly and take him ouside to "paint" the snow with his spray bottle. Children will also enjoy using brushes and liquid tempera paint to paint the snow.

Teddy Swing

Rope, heavy string, or ribbon
Teddy bear or favorite stuffed animal

Tie one end of a length of rope, heavy string, or ribbon around the waist of your child's favorite teddy bear or other stuffed animal. Tie the other end of the rope to a tree branch so that teddy is about 2 feet off the ground. Your child will have fun pushing his teddy to make him swing.

Window Painting

Adding a little dish detergent to the fingerpaint makes cleanup easier!

Fingerpaint
Dish detergent (optional)
Wet paintbrush or Q-Tip (optional)

On a warm day outdoors, let your child fingerpaint on the outside of a glass patio door or low window. When the paint dries, use a wet paintbrush or Q-Tip dipped in water to make a design on the paint. Cleaning up with a sponge and bucket of water or garden hose can be part of the fun.

Crayon Slide

If you have a slide in your backyard (or a small one indoors), this activity will add a new dimension to sliding fun.

Slide
Newsprint or long length of paper
Tape
Crayons

Tape a length of newsprint to your child's slide. Give him one or two crayons (perhaps one for each hand) and have him slide down the slide, holding the crayons to the paper as he goes. He will enjoy seeing the squiggly lines and designs he's made. Change colors and keep sliding until your child tires of this activity.

If you like, bundle up three or four (or more) crayons with a rubber band for a different effect.

Rope Games

This activity is good for either indoor or outdoor play.

Long rope

Lay a long rope in a zigzag pattern in the grass or on your deck. See if your child can walk on the rope. Lay the rope in a straight line like a tightrope and have your child hold out his arms to balance himself as he walks. With the rope still lying straight, ask your child to think of how many ways he can go over it: walk across it, hop over it (on one or two feet), jump across it, crawl across it, or any other way he can think of.

CHAPTER 6
Out and About

"Children are a great comfort in your old age and they help
you reach it faster, too."
—*Lionel M. Kauffman*

Most children, no matter what their age, would rather be
playing and moving about than sitting still for an extended
period of time. Also, toddlers are fairly limited in their lan-
guage skills and ability to play games and carry out independent activities. For these reasons, long car rides and waits in
the doctor's office can be especially frustrating for those with
a toddler in tow.

There are, however, simple things you can do to help your
child through these challenging situations. Provide her with
her very own Busy Bag (see Chapter 1) and fill it with toddler-
appropriate items. Bring along her favorite book, toy, or snack
to help her through times when you're forced to sit and wait.
Sing songs, recite nursery rhymes, and learn some simple finger plays to keep her attention (see Chapter 7).

The ideas in this chapter are great for those times when
your toddler just has to sit. The simple games and activities
will help keep her entertained and happy, and many may
become favorites for other times as well.

Where Is It?

As you're driving in the car, name things that you see and ask your toddler to point to them (for example, "Where is the tree?") If you're waiting in a place where your child can move around, ask her to walk over to the object you name.

Color of the Day

Before you set out on a car trip, choose a "Color of the Day." As you're driving in the car, shopping at the grocery store, or waiting at the doctor's office, help your toddler point to and identify all the things she sees that match the color you've chosen.

Car Book

Old magazines
Scissors
Construction paper
Glue
Clear contact paper
Hole punch
Ribbon

Look through old magazines for pictures of cars or other vehicles. Cut out the pictures and glue them to pieces of construction paper. Protect the pages by covering them with clear contact paper. Punch two or three holes in the left margin of each page, then thread ribbon through the holes to make a book. (If you like, use a ring binder or staple the pages together.)

Give your child her car book to look through as you drive along. Ask her questions as she looks at the pages. For example, "Can you find a blue car?" or "Can you find a truck?" and so on.

Nursery Rhyme Fun

As you drive along, recite a familiar nursery rhyme or sing a familiar song to your child. When you get to a rhyming word, stop and see if your toddler can say or sing the correct word. For example, say, "Hickory, dickory, dock, the mouse ran up the _____" or "Little Jack Horner sat in a _____" or "Jack, be nimble, Jack be quick, Jack jump over the _____."

What Would You Be?

You can encourage your older two- or three-year-old to use her imagination by playing games such as this. Ask your child, "If you could spend one day as an animal, which one would you be?" and "What do you think your day might be like?" You may want to give your child some examples or start the game off yourself, pretending to be a dog digging for a bone, or a baby bird in the nest waiting for Mommy to return.

Ask a Question

While riding in the car or waiting for your meal at a restaurant, take a few minutes to ask your child some questions. Try to avoid yes/no questions and encourage your child to give reasons for her answers. Some of her responses may be hilarious, but you'll be surprised at what you can learn about your child if you take the time to really listen to the answers she gives. Here are a few questions to start you off:

- Who is your best friend?
- Where does money come from?
- What is the best thing about Daddy (or Mommy)?
- What is the nicest thing that has ever happened to you?
- What is your favorite thing to do?
- When does God sleep?

Sandpaper Play

This is a clean, quiet activity that travels well. Store sandpaper and yarn in a Ziploc bag and have it handy for a long car ride or whenever you need something quick for your child to do.

Coarse sandpaper
Yarn in various colors

Cut various colors of yarn into different lengths. Show your toddler how the yarn sticks to the sandpaper. She will enjoy creating a design, pulling it off, and starting over again.

Stop and Go

Red and green construction paper
Scissors
Tape
Straw

Cut two circles from the red and green construction paper.
Tape a straw to the back of each circle, leaving enough straw
extending below the circle for your child to hold on to. Give
your child the circles to hold in the car.

As you drive up to a red light, say to your child, "I'm stop-
ping now because the light is red. Can you hold up your red
light?" When the light turns green, say, "I'm starting to drive
now because the light is green. Can you hold up your green
light?" If you like, refer to your child's red and green lights as
red and green circles to reinforce the concept of shape.

You can also play this game by cutting a stop sign from red
construction paper. Tape a straw to the back, give it to your
child, and ask her to hold her sign up every time you stop.

Toddler Brag Book

This little homemade photo album slips easily into a diaper bag and comes in handy during long car rides or waits in a restaurant or doctor's office.

Photos of friends, family, pets, and your toddler
Construction paper
Glue
Clear contact paper
Scissors
Hole punch
Ribbon

Glue photos of your child and her friends, family, and pets to pieces of construction paper. Cover them with clear contact paper and cut to size, leaving a border of at least ½ inch around the photo. Punch two holes in the left margin of each page. Thread ribbon through the holes to make a "brag book." Your child will enjoy looking at this over and over.

If you like, use a small store-bought photo album (one photo per page) instead of making one with construction and contact paper.

Shopping List

This word game may be beyond most one- and two-year-olds, but older two- and three-year-olds will love it.

As you drive along, say to your child, "I went to the store and I bought carrots, cabbage, and cream. What else did I buy?" Your child must add items to your shopping list that begin with the same sound as the items you have named. You can tell your child the rule for adding items (that they must begin with the same sound), or let older children figure it out for themselves. If they try to add something that doesn't begin with the same sound, tell them, "No, that wasn't on my list." They'll probably guess the rule after a few tries, but if they have trouble, keep adding items to your list until they understand.

Felt Faces

Cardboard
Scissors
Felt
Glue
Pen or marker
Ziploc bag, diaper-wipe container,
  or small shoebox for storage

Cut several oval shapes out of cardboard. Trace around these shapes on pieces of felt (since these will be faces, felt in a variety of skin colors is desirable, but brightly colored felt will work, too). Cut out the felt shapes you have traced and glue them to the cardboard ovals. Cut additional facial features from the felt in a variety of colors. These features should include eyes, noses, mouths (smiling and frowning), ears (with and without earrings, if you like), and hair. Older children may enjoy using additional features such as eyebrows, eyeglasses, mustaches, and so on.

Place the felt pieces (oval face shapes and facial features) in a Ziploc bag, empty diaper-wipe container, or small shoebox. This makes a clean and quiet take-along game to play in the car or while you're waiting.

What Would Happen If . . . ?

This is a great activity to promote creative thinking in young children. Ask your child some "What would happen if . . ." questions. For example, "What would happen if the dinosaurs came back?" or "What would happen if cars could fly?" or "What would happen if broccoli tasted like chocolate?" or "What would happen if all the trees were red?" and so on.

Take-Along Tape

Tape recorder with microphone
Cassette tape

Spend some time on your own making a tape for your toddler. Include familiar household sounds, sounds of animals, outdoor sounds, voices that the child will recognize, and so on. As you drive along, play the tape for your toddler and ask her to guess the sounds she hears.

As a variation, choose a story that your child is familiar with and read it on tape. As you read, make some mistakes, changing words in obvious places throughout the story. Have your child listen to the tape and pick out the errors.

CHAPTER 7

Nursery Rhymes and Finger Plays

"There never was a child so lovely but his mother was glad to get him asleep."
—*Ralph Waldo Emerson*

Nursery rhymes and finger plays can be used in many different circumstances. You can use them on walks with your toddler or driving in the car. They will amuse your child at changing time or while he waits for his meal in his highchair. Sing or say the rhymes and finger plays as you rock in the rocking chair or as your child plays in his bath. Nursery rhymes and finger plays are appropriate just about anytime and anyplace.

In her book *The Baby Games* (Stoddart Publishing Company, 1988), Elaine Martin says, "A common criticism of traditional nursery fare is that it is violent. Much of it is violent, aggressive, and full of surprises. While recognizing human gentleness, there is also an acknowledgement of the all-too-real capacity for human evil." While Martin goes on to contend that the nature of such rhymes allows us to resolve underlying conflicts in our lives in an appropriate way, many parents will not be comfortable reciting such nursery rhymes to their children. A book such as *The New Adventures of Mother Goose* by Bruce Lansky (Meadowbrook Press, 1993), and the rhymes and finger plays that follow provide a gentle alternative to frightening nursery rhymes.

To help you learn the words of any song or rhyme you're not familiar with, begin by reciting two lines at a time, repeating those lines throughout the day until you know them by heart. Add another two lines and continue in this way until the whole rhyme is memorized. Posting one or two unfamiliar rhymes around your baby's change table, on the wall next to the rocking chair, or on the kitchen wall close to his highchair will also help you learn them. You'll know them well after reading and saying them to your toddler several times.

Slowly, Slowly

Use your hands to mime the actions suggested by the words, or just use the rhyme as a tickling game with baby.

Slowly, slowly, very slowly
Creeps the garden snail.
Slowly, slowly, very slowly
Up the wooden rail.

Quickly, quickly, very quickly
Runs the little mouse.
Quickly, quickly, very quickly
Round about the house.

Round and Round the Garden

For the second verse, repeat the actions given for the first.

Round and round the garden (Run your index finger
around baby's palm.)
Went the Teddy Bear,
One step, two steps, (Jump your finger up his arm.)
Tickle under there. (Tickle him under his arm.)

Round and round the haystack,
Went the little mouse,
One step, two steps,
In his little house.

Grandmother's Glasses

Make appropriate actions to fit the words as you say them. For glasses, join the thumb and forefinger on each hand. Use a higher voice for Grandmother, a deeper voice for Grandfather.

These are Grandmother's glasses,
This is Grandmother's hat;
Grandmother claps her hands like this,
And folds them in her lap.

These are Grandfather's glasses,
This is Grandfather's hat;
This is the way he folds his arms,
And has a little nap.

Two Little Eyes

Point to each feature as it is mentioned.

Two little eyes to look around,
Two little ears to hear each sound,
One little nose to smell what's sweet,
One little mouth that likes to eat.

Mix a Pancake

Mime each action as you say it.

Mix a pancake,
Stir a pancake,
Pop it in the pan.

Fry the pancake,
Toss the pancake,
Catch it if you can!

Here's a Ball for Baby

Here's a ball for baby, (Make a ball with cupped hands.)
Big and soft and round.
Here is baby's hammer, (Hammer with one fist.)
See how he can pound.

Here is baby's music, (Clap hands.)
Clapping, clapping, so.
Here are baby's soldiers, (Hold fingers up straight.)
Standing in a row.

Here is his umbrella, (Hold hands above head.)
To keep our baby dry.
Here is baby's cradle, (Fold arms together and rock them.)
To rock-a-baby-bye.

I Hear Thunder

This is sung to the tune of "Frère Jacques," or "Are You Sleeping?"

I hear thunder, I hear thunder, (Drum feet on the floor.)
Hark, don't you, hark, don't you? (Pretend to listen.)
Pitter-patter raindrops, (Flutter your fingers for raindrops.)
Pitter-patter raindrops,
I'm wet through, (Shake your body vigorously.)
So are you! (Point to your child.)

Snowflakes

Mime the actions suggested by the words.

Softly, softly falling so,
This is how the snowflakes go.
Pitter-patter, pitter-patter,
Pit pit pat,
Down go the raindrops
On my hat.

Five Little Monkeys

Mime the actions of each monkey and use your fingers to indicate the number of monkeys as you say this rhyme.

Five little monkeys walked along the shore;
One went a-sailing,
Then there were four.

Four little monkeys climbed up a tree;
One of them tumbled down,
Then there were three.

Three little monkeys found a pot of glue;
One got stuck in it,
Then there were two.

Two little monkeys found a currant bun;
One ran away with it,
Then there was one.

One little monkey cried all afternoon,
So they put him in an airplane
And sent him to the moon.

Walking through the Jungle

Pretend to walk very carefully through the jungle and mime the actions to suggest each animal. It's easy to make up more verses for this rhyme.

Walking through the jungle,
What did I see?
A big lion roaring
At me, me, me!

Walking through the jungle,
What did I see?
A baby monkey laughing
At me, me, me!

Walking through the jungle,
What did I see?
A slippery snake hissing
At me, me, me!

Ten Little Gentlemen

Use your fingers to represent the gentlemen in this rhyme.
When the door closes at the end, be sure to give a big clap.

Ten little gentlemen, standing in a row.
Bow, little gentlemen, bow down low;
Walk, little gentlemen, right across the floor,
And don't forget, gentlemen, to please close the door.

Five Little Mice

Use the fingers of one hand for the mice and the other hand
for the cat. Continue each verse with one less mouse until
there are no little mice scampering back.

Five little mice came out to play,
Gathering up crumbs on their way;
Out came a pussycat, sleek and black
Four little mice went scampering back.

Four little mice came out to play . . .

Little Pussycats

One, two, three, four, (Hold up four fingers from the right
  hand and count them.)
These little pussycats came to my door.
They just stood there and said "Good day," (Make the fingers
  bow on "Good day.")
And then they tiptoed right away. (Walk the fingers away over
  the front of the body and behind the left shoulder.)

Marching Song

This song is sung to the tune of "Twinkle, Twinkle, Little
Star." March around the room, either in separate directions
or following the leader, as you sing it.

See the soldiers in the street,
Hear the marching of their feet;
They are singing as they go,
Marching, marching, to and fro.
See the soldiers in the street,
Hear the marching of their feet.

CHAPTER 8

Early Learning Fun

"Before I got married I had six theories about bringing up children. Now I have six children and no theories."
—*Lord Rochester*

The name of this chapter seems to imply that the activities contained within are the only ones in this book from which your child will learn. In reality, children are learning all the time. Toddlers learn with their hands, their ears, their noses, their mouths, and their feet. They learn by doing, looking, touching, smelling, tasting, banging, dropping, and listening. A toddler's play is her pathway to learning.

Seen in that light, most of the activities in this book provide learning opportunities for toddlers: building with blocks; playing with mud, sand, and water; swinging, sliding, and running outdoors; moving to music; and crafting with paper, paints, and glue. All these activities help your child learn and help her make sense of the world around her.

The best way to optimize your child's ability to learn is to create a stimulating environment for her. Provide her with lots of exposure to interesting things to see, touch, and hear. Recite rhymes, sing, and play finger games as you change her diaper (post one or two new rhymes or songs by the changing table to help you learn them). Look through magazines for colorful pictures of everyday objects; paste them onto cardboard, cover them with clear contact paper, and display them on the wall by the crib, changing table, or highchair. And most importantly, talk, talk, talk to your child about everything you're doing.

Don't be in a rush to push academics. Young children—toddlers in particular—must spend lots of time developing their motor skills in order to make academic learning possible and productive. Activities that develop gross motor skills include running, jumping, hopping, dancing, and playing with balls, pull toys, push toys, riding toys, climbing toys, swings, and slides. Activities that develop fine motor skills include filling and emptying boxes and containers and playing with nesting or stacking toys, simple wooden jigsaw puzzles, shape sorters, and blocks. You'll find ideas for these types of activities throughout this book.

The activities in this chapter deal primarily with those skills we think of as "academic": sorting, matching, classifying, and recognizing patterns, shapes, colors, and so on. All these skills are required in order for a child to learn basic math and reading skills. But your toddler can learn these skills in any number of ways. For instance, playing with Duplo is a great way to learn basic math skills: A toddler can sort pieces by color and size, build towers and compare their sizes, count pieces, make patterns, and so on. These are essential activities for math readiness.

Many of the ideas in this chapter are not for everyone. Some will require a fair amount of time to prepare, making them more suitable for a day-care or preschool setting where more than one child will benefit. If you do choose to spend time assembling these activities, be sure to protect them as best you can. Covering with clear contact paper makes cards and other items more durable. Storage is also important. Shoeboxes and diaper-wipe containers are great for storage, and they stack nicely on shelves or in cupboards. Sets of cards should be zipped into individual Ziploc bags and stored in a large plastic container with a cover. Sets of cards relating to similar concepts—colors or shapes, for example—should be stored together.

Can You Find Your Knee?

Most of us play this game informally with our children at one time or another. Very young children often easily point to their eyes, noses, mouths, and ears when asked to do so. Encourage them to identify less common body parts including nostrils, eyelashes, fingernails, lips, throat, wrists, knees, ankles, and so on. This will stimulate the development of memory and vocabulary as well as their ability to recognize parts of the body.

Animal Sort

Gather together all the stuffed animals you can find. Help your toddler sort them by color or by size (using words like *small, smaller, smallest, big, bigger,* and *biggest*). Older children may want to sort them by the type of sound they make (loud, soft) or by their habitat (jungle, forest, farm).

Pocket Matching

This is a fun game for toddlers, but takes a while to prepare. If you've already made the Memory game on page 187, use the Memory cards for handkerchiefs and matching gift-wrap for pockets.

Gift-wrap or fabric in 4–6
  different patterns and colors
Scissors
Posterboard, file folder, or
  large piece of cardboard
Glue
Clear contact paper
Utility knife
Small index cards or pieces of
  cardboard, posterboard, or heavy paper

Cut a pocket from each piece of gift-wrap. Glue the pockets to a large piece of posterboard, leaving the top of the pocket open. Cover the posterboard with clear contact paper. Slit open the top of each pocket with a utility knife. Cut gift-wrap rectangles that will fit in the pockets. (These will be the hand-kerchiefs.) Glue them to small index cards and cover both sides with clear contact paper. Your toddler will have fun matching the handkerchiefs to the pockets. Store the hand-kerchiefs in an envelope or Ziploc bag attached to the back of the posterboard.

Short and Tall

Paper towel rolls
Scissors
Colorful contact paper or gift-wrap (optional)

Cut paper towel rolls into several different sizes. If you like, cover them with colorful contact paper. Encourage your child to stand the rolls up in order from shortest to tallest. Store the rolls in an empty coffee can, shoebox, or diaper-wipe container when not in use.

Pompom Fun

Pompoms in various sizes and colors

Purchase pompoms in a variety of colors and sizes from a fabric or craft store. For very young children, start with no more than three colors or sizes. Use several sizes of pompoms in one color and encourage your child to sort them by size. Use one size of pompoms in several colors and ask your child to sort them by color. Store pompoms in a Ziploc bag when not in use.

Spools of thread also work well for sorting and matching. Use two spools of each color in at least three different colors.

Picture Box

This takes a bit of time to prepare. Try starting with just a few
pictures and adding to your collection as time permits.

File or recipe box
Index cards to fit the box
Magazine pictures
Scissors
Glue
Clear contact paper

Cut interesting, colorful pictures of familiar objects from
magazines. Glue them onto the index cards and cover with
clear contact paper. Place the cards in the file or recipe box.
Your toddler will enjoy looking at the pictures by herself or
with you. If you use 4-inch by 6-inch index cards, they will fit
in a small photo album, an easy item to slip into most diaper
bags. Take it with you on a long car ride, talking about each
picture as you look at it.

You can maintain your Picture Box as your child grows,
adding new pictures and perhaps dividing the pictures into
categories such as flowers, animals, people, and so on. Your
Picture Box will eventually be a great sorting game, too.

Clothespin Colors

Spring-type clothespins
Paint (optional)
Colored dot stickers (or use white and color them yourself)
Empty coffee can

Paint five or six clothespins in different colors to match the colored dot stickers, or decorate each clothespin with additional colored dot stickers. Stick colored dot stickers evenly around the top of the coffee can, leaving some space in between. Show your toddler how to clip each clothespin just above the matching colored dot. Store the clothespins inside the coffee can when not in use.

Picture Sort

If the cutting and gluing aspect of preparing this activity will take more time than you have, use two sets of matching stickers instead.

Metal lids from frozen-juice cans
Double set of pictures (either photographs or from a
  magazine)
Glue
Clear contact paper
Magnets (optional)
Plastic container, shoebox, or diaper-wipe container

Cut a double set of pictures of family and friends (or pictures from two identical magazines) into a round shape that will fit the lid of a frozen-juice can. Glue the pictures onto the lids and cover with clear contact paper. (You should have two sets of lids exactly the same.) Have your child sort the lids into pairs by matching the two pictures that are the same. If you like, glue magnets to the backs of the lids and make this a refrigerator or cookie-sheet activity.

Store the lids in a plastic container, shoebox, or diaper-wipe container with a slit cut in the top. Your toddler will enjoy dropping the lids into the opening to put the game away.

Egg Sort

Even toddlers too young for sorting and matching activities
will have fun playing with these colorful plastic eggs.

12 plastic Easter eggs
Glue gun
Egg carton

Purchase a dozen inexpensive plastic Easter eggs in three to
six different colors. Use a glue gun to glue the two parts of
each egg together. Encourage your child to sort the eggs by
color. If you like, color the compartments of an egg carton to
match the eggs; have your child place each egg in a compartment of the same color. Store the eggs in the egg carton
when not in use.

Spoon Match

2 sets of measuring spoons

Mix up two sets of measuring spoons. Encourage your child to
match up two spoons of the same size. Use only one set of
spoons and have your child order them from smallest to largest.

More Fun with Pictures

If you don't have any old calendars with appropriate pictures on hand, check out bookstores in January when they're selling calendars at big discounts. They're a great source of big, beautiful pictures in many different themes.

Old calendars with pictures of recognizable objects
   (dogs, cats, cars, and so on)
Construction paper
Scissors
Glue
Clear contact paper

Cut out several pictures, mount them on construction paper, and cover with clear contact paper. If the pictures are a standard size, you can put them in a three-ring binder; otherwise, store them in a box or file folder. Your child will love to look at the pictures. As she gets older, she'll enjoy mixing them up and sorting them out (all the dogs in one pile, cats in another, and so on).

Large and Small

5–6 pairs of objects that are similar in every way except size
(adult/child socks, long/short pencils, dinner/lunch plates)

Holding up the two matching items, ask your child which one
is smaller. Be sure to use terms such as bigger, smaller, shorter,
and longer in your everyday conversation to draw attention to
the size of objects around you.

Pasta Sort

Dried pasta in 2–3 (or more) different shapes
Bowl or plastic container

Combine two or three different shapes of dried pasta in a bowl
or plastic container. Pick out one piece and ask your toddler
to find a piece that matches. If you like, have several small
containers on hand and ask your toddler to sort the pasta into
the containers. For colorful pasta, dye the pasta beforehand
using the Pasta Dye recipe on page 363.

Parking Game

This simple matching game is lots of fun. Even toddlers with
no concept of color will enjoy parking the cars in the garages,
whether they match or not.

Small boxes (shoeboxes work well, as do some cereal boxes)
3–4 toy cars in different colors
Scissors
Construction paper
Glue
Paint (optional)
Colored contact paper (optional)

In one side of each box cut a garage door big enough to fit
a toy car. Cover each box with colored construction paper,
matching the colors of the paper to the cars. (If you like, use
colored contact paper or paint the boxes instead.) Turn each
box upside down so the bottom of the box is the roof of the
garage. Encourage your child to park each car in the garage
of the same color. Store the garages and cars in a larger box
or plastic container when not in use.

More Pompom Fun

Pompoms in various sizes and colors
Clear plastic drinking cups
Permanent marker

Use a permanent marker to make dots on the front of a clear plastic cup. One cup should have one dot, another two dots, the next three dots, and so on. You can mark as many cups as you feel your child is able to match. Give her an assortment of pompoms and show her how to drop the same number of pompoms as dots into the cup. If you like, use beans, large nuts, golf tees, large plastic paper clips, small spools of thread, or other small objects in place of pompoms. Store the cups and objects in a small box or diaper-wipe container when not in use.

Find the Color

Tell your child, "I see the color blue. Can you find it?" As you count down from ten to zero, your child must then run to touch something that includes the color you have named before you finish counting.

Memory

This is a great way to recycle gift-wrap. You can also make this a seasonal activity by using gift-wrap in holiday patterns or cutting the cards into shapes such as winter mittens, hearts, or Easter eggs.

Gift-wrap in a variety of patterns and colors
3-inch by 5-inch index cards
Glue
Scissors
Clear contact paper
Clothespins (optional)

Cut gift-wrap into 3-inch by 5-inch rectangles, making two rectangles from each pattern or color of paper. Glue each rectangle to a small index card. Cover both sides of the index card with clear contact paper and trim the edges. Make five to ten pairs of cards (more for older children).

Very young children will enjoy simply handling and looking at the cards. Gradually encourage them to lay the cards out faceup and try to clip the matching pairs together with clothespins. Older toddlers and preschoolers will enjoy playing a game of Memory, where all cards are laid out face down and each player takes a turn trying to turn over a matching pair.

Store the cards in a Ziploc bag. If you use clothespins with this game, store both clothespins and cards in a shoebox or diaper-wipe container when not in use.

Mail Carrier

Construction paper
Scissors
Shoeboxes or plastic baskets
Clear contact paper

Cut circles, squares, and triangles out of various colors of
construction paper. Cover the shapes with clear contact paper.
Tape one of each shape (if sorting by shapes) or each color (if
sorting by colors) to a shoebox or small plastic basket. Give
the remaining shapes to your child and have her play Mail
Carrier—delivering all the shapes or colors to their proper
mailboxes. You can also play this game with Duplo, wooden
blocks, or other items you may have around the house. Try
varying the criteria, sorting by big and small, hard and soft,
and so on.

If using baskets, they will stack nicely in a cupboard or on
a shelf when not in use. Store the cards in a Ziploc bag with
the baskets.

Color Game

Help your child learn her colors and sharpen her listening
skills at the same time.

Objects of various colors

Give your child various directions by color (for example, "Put
the red bear on the table," "Pick up the blue car," and "Bring me
the yellow book"). You can also do this with actions based on
the color of your child's clothes: "If you are wearing green, you
may sit down," or "If you are wearing orange, clap your hands."

Cars and Colors

Toy cars
Construction paper

Start with two cars in two different colors, such as red and
blue. Have construction paper in red and blue, too. Play with
the cars for a while, then "park" each car on the construction
paper of the same color. Be sure to talk about the cars and
their colors as you play. Play with the cars some more, then
see if your child can park each car on the matching paper.
Add another color as each is mastered.

Color Match

Construction paper
Black marker
Crayons

Give your child a crayon that matches the color of each piece of construction paper. (For very young children, start with only two colors.) If you like, use a black marker to write the name of the color on each sheet of construction paper. Hold up one of the pieces of paper and ask her to pick out the crayon of the same color, or place the papers and crayons on the table and have her match them up that way. Be sure to use the color names as you do this (for example, "I have a red piece of paper. Can you find the red crayon that will match my paper?").

Color Cards

Construction paper
Black marker
Scissors
Clear contact paper

Make up two sets of cards from construction paper. Start with only a few colors, working your way up to the nine basic colors (red, green, blue, brown, yellow, orange, purple, black, and white). If you like, write the names of each color on the card. Cover the cards with clear contact paper. Spread the cards out on a table and begin by picking up one of the cards and saying, "I have a red card. Can you hand me the other red card?" After a while, your child will enjoy matching the cards all by herself. Store the cards in a small Ziploc bag when not in use.

Color Hunt

Help your toddler learn her colors by going on a color hunt together.

Paper or plastic bags
Hunting hats (optional)

Begin your color hunt by putting on your hunting hats and picking a color to hunt. To begin, show your child an object that represents the color you're looking for, name the color, then put it in the bag. Do this two or three times, then let your child be the hunter. When you're finished, empty your bags and name the items together (red sock, red ball, red cup). You can also hunt for colors (without collecting objects) at the grocery store or when you're driving along together.

Object Matchup

Paper
Household objects
Pencil, pen, or marker
Clear contact paper
Scissors
Box or bag

Gather several common household objects, such as a spoon, cookie cutter, or key (something with a recognizable shape). Place each object on a separate piece of paper and trace around it. Cover the sheets of paper with clear contact paper. Put all the objects inside a box or bag and spread the pages with the outlined shapes on the table or floor. Have your child remove an object from the box or bag and match it to its outline.

Store the objects and their outlines in a shoebox or diaper-wipe container when not in use.

Search and Sort

Make sure the stones you use for this activity are large enough not to pose a choking hazard.

48 stones (plus a few extras for those that get lost)
4 empty egg cartons
Paint or spray paint in 4 different colors

Paint twelve stones per color and let dry; if using tempera paint, you may want to finish with a clear acrylic spray. If you like, paint each of the egg cartons a different color. Give your child the stones and the egg cartons. She will have fun sorting the stones and storing them in the egg cartons. You can also hide the stones in her sandbox for her to dig up and collect in a bucket.

Colorful Clothespins

Craft-type clothespins (without springs)
3 empty coffee cans
Paint, crayons, or markers
Construction paper or colored contact paper

Paint or color 5–6 clothespins in the primary colors (red, yellow, and blue). Cover each coffee can with a different primary color, using construction paper or colored contact paper. Encourage your older toddler to match the colors as she places the clothespins around the rim of the can. You can also cut a small hole in the plastic lid of the can and have her drop the clothespins through the lid. Store the clothespins in the covered coffee cans when not in use.

Apple Seed Count

Apple
Knife
Paint (optional)
Paper (optional)

Cut an apple in half and remove all the apple seeds. Count the seeds with your child. Eat the apple for a snack or dip it in paint and onto paper to make an apple print.

Paper Plate Numbers

20 small paper plates
Black marker
Stickers or dots

Make up a matching set of paper plates with numbers from one to ten. Put one sticker on the edge of each of two plates, and write the numeral 1 and/or the word *one* in the center of the plate. Make pairs with the rest of the numerals in the same way. You can use this as a hands-on matching activity or just display the plates on a wall in your child's bedroom or wherever she spends time during the day.

Color Cube

Empty milk cartons
  (any size will do)
Construction or contact
  paper in six different colors

Tape
Scissors
Glue
Clear contact paper

Choose two milk cartons the same size. Measure the base of one carton and mark a cutting line that same distance up the side of the carton. Cut along the line. Cut the other carton in the same way. You should now have two open-ended cubes. Push one cube open-end-down into the other cube. Tape around the cut edges. Cut squares to fit one side of the cube out of six different colors of construction paper. Glue one square to each side of the cube. Cover with clear contact paper for durability.

You can use your color cube in many different ways:

- Have your child throw the cube up in the air; when it lands, ask her to bring you something that matches the color on top of the cube.
- Cut squares of construction paper in the same colors as the cube and cover with clear contact paper. When she tosses the cube in the air, have her hand you the color card that matches the color on top of the cube.
- Match the colors on the cube to crayons, toys, or Duplo.
- Come up with matching activities of your own. You can also make a shape cube and matching cards and play in the same way.

Turntable Fun

Double set of stickers, shapes, or colors
Glue
Scissors
Construction paper
Clear contact paper
Plastic kitchen turntable

Use a double set of stickers or cut a double set of simple shapes or colors from construction paper. If using stickers, stick one set of stickers on small squares of construction paper. Cover the construction paper with clear contact paper. Stick the other set of stickers, shapes, or colors around the outer edge of a plastic kitchen turntable. Slowly move the turntable and have your child match the shapes, colors, or stickers in her hand with the ones on the turntable. If matching colors, try matching a crayon to the color on the turntable.

Beanbag Toss

Large sheet of paper
Markers or paints
Beanbag

On a large sheet of paper, draw or paint several large shapes in different colors (or cut shapes out of construction paper and lay them on the floor). Have your child stand a few feet away and toss a beanbag onto the shapes. Have her identify the color and/or shape the beanbag landed on. As she becomes more skilled, ask her to aim for a certain shape (for example, "Let's try for the red square this time. Oops! You hit the yellow circle!").

Alphabet Sand

Sand, salt, or sugar
Metal pie plate

Pour sand, salt, or sugar into a metal pie plate. Your child can learn her letters by making their shapes with her index finger in the sand. Start with simple letters like O, C, V, or X. Avoid salt if your child has a cut on her finger; avoid sugar if you think she may eat more than she spells!

Tape Shapes

Masking tape or colorful tape

Use masking tape or colorful tape to make several different shapes on the floor. Call out different movements, such as "Crawl to the square," "Hop to the circle," or "Run to the triangle."

If you like, make a Shape Cube (see Color Cube, page 197) with the same shapes on it as you have taped on the floor. Throw the Shape Cube into the air and when it lands, have your child move to the same shape as is displayed on the top of the cube.

Practical Math

Give your child the opportunity to develop math skills in her everyday world. Count everything with your child: steps as you climb them, toys as you pick them up, cups as you set the table. Take your child on household counting assignments. You can count the number of doors in your house (including closets). Count out loud with your child as you match napkins to place mats, forks to spoons, and so on.

Find the Oddball

8½-inch by 11-inch paper, cut in half lengthwise
Markers, shapes cut out of construction paper, or stickers
Clear contact paper
Scissors

On each strip of paper make a set of pictures or symbols that are all the same except for one (for example, five happy faces, one sad face; five cat stickers, one dog sticker; five triangles, one circle; and so on). Cover with clear contact paper. Ask your child to find the oddball. Older children can explain how it differs from the others in the set.

Store the strips in a large Ziploc bag when not in use.

Shape Matchup

Construction paper in 4 different colors
Scissors
Clear contact paper

Cut out two sets of the four basic geometric shapes (circle, triangle, square, rectangle) from construction paper, using a different color for each shape. Cover with clear contact paper. Give one set to your child. Hold up one shape from your set and ask her if she can find the matching shape from her set, being sure to call the shape by its name as you do. ("I have a circle. Can you find a circle, too?") You can also mix up both sets on the table and have your child pick out the matching shapes. If you think your child is matching by color or by associating a certain shape with a certain color, try it again with a new set of shapes in different colors, or make the shapes all the same color.

Store the shapes in a Ziploc bag when not in use.

Playdough Numbers

Construction paper or white or colored copier paper
Broad-tip marker
Clear contact paper
Playdough

Use a broad-tip marker to write the numerals 0 to 10, using one piece of paper for each numeral. Cover each piece of paper with clear contact paper. Show your child how to roll playdough into ropes and shape the playdough on each piece of paper to match the shape of the numeral.

Sock Matchup

This will help your child match up her socks and learn her numbers at the same time.

Permanent laundry marker
Socks

Number each pair of your child's socks with a permanent laundry marker. You can have her match up her socks as you fold the laundry, or place them in her drawer and have her match them as she wears them.

Number Cube

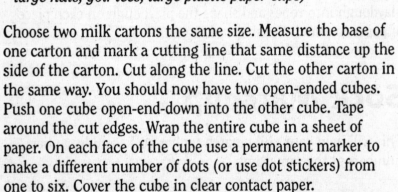

Empty milk cartons (any size will do)
Tape
Construction paper
Clear contact paper
Scissors
Permanent marker
6 small objects for counting (pompoms, beans,
*   large nuts, golf tees, large plastic paper clips)*

Choose two milk cartons the same size. Measure the base of
one carton and mark a cutting line that same distance up the
side of the carton. Cut along the line. Cut the other carton in
the same way. You should now have two open-ended cubes.
Push one cube open-end-down into the other cube. Tape
around the cut edges. Wrap the entire cube in a sheet of
paper. On each face of the cube use a permanent marker to
make a different number of dots (or use dot stickers) from
one to six. Cover the cube in clear contact paper.

   Give your child six small objects to count with. Show her
how to throw the die in the air and count out the same number of objects as dots on the top of the cube. If you like, substitute raisins, small pieces of cereal, or chocolate chips for
the objects to count with. Count out the correct number,
then eat them!

CHAPTER 9
Music and Movement

"The commonest fallacy among women is that simply having children makes one a mother—which is as absurd as believing that having a piano makes one a musician."
—*Sydney J. Harris*

Anyone who has ever watched a baby's reaction to music knows that babies seem to be born with a sense of music and rhythm. Even before they're old enough to walk, many will bob their heads and wiggle their little bodies when lively music comes on. Once they can walk, just try to stop them from jiggling and dancing anytime, anywhere they hear a snappy beat.

Often the first music your child hears will come from you. Don't worry if you can't carry a tune; your voice is the most beautiful one he hears. Sing as you rock him, walk him, carry him, change him, bathe him, and play with him. If you don't know many songs, borrow a few tapes or CDs of children's songs from the library, or buy them for your own collection.

Children also seem to have a natural instinct for movement. Once a child can walk, run, jump, and climb, there are many days when it seems that is all he wants to do. Movement activities are important because they help your child develop his gross motor skills. Moving to music is equally important, because it helps your child experience movement as it relates to music and rhythm.

Listening to, moving to, and making music should be part of every day for you and your child. These activities have many benefits, but for most children they are just plain fun!

Button Tap

Large buttons with 2 holes
Rubber bands
Empty cooking pots
Small gloves (optional)

Insert the looped ends of a rubber band into the two holes of
a large button. Bring the looped ends together and slide onto
your child's finger. Put a few of these on each hand and let
your child tap out some music on an upside-down pot.

For a variation, sew small buttons onto the fingers of a
small glove. Place the glove on your child's hand and let him
tap around the house.

Strumming Fun

Corrugated cardboard
Spoon

Show your child how to strum a spoon across the ridges on a
piece of corrugated cardboard for a neat sound.

Paper Bag Shaker

Paper bag
Rice or dried beans
Ribbon or rubber band

Make a simple shaker for your toddler by putting a small amount of rice or dried beans into a paper bag (you may want to decorate the bag with markers or stickers first). Tie the bag securely with a piece of ribbon or a rubber band. This simple shaker can add a lot of enjoyment to your songs and dance.

Simple Shaker

Empty film canisters or small plastic bottles
Small rocks, beads, buttons, or popcorn kernels

Place a few rocks, beads, buttons, popcorn kernels, or other small objects into an empty film canister or other small plastic container. Glue the lid on securely to prevent a possible choking hazard.

Coffee Can Drum

Empty coffee can with 2 plastic lids
Contact paper or your child's artwork
Glue
Pencil
Empty thread spool

You can create a drum for your child by cutting the bottom out of a coffee can and covering the can with contact paper (or letting your child draw a picture on some paper and gluing it around the can). Glue plastic lids on each end of the can. Create a drumstick by gluing the lead end of a pencil into the hole of an empty thread spool.

For a variation, an empty paper towel roll and an empty oatmeal box will make a soft but authentic drum for your toddler.

Toddler Triangle

You may want to cover the sharp ends of the nails with tape before using them.

2 large (5-inch) nails
String

Tie a string around the head of one of the large nails. While holding onto the string, tap the "triangle" with the other nail.

Tiny Tambourine

2 small aluminum tart pans (about 3 inches in diameter)
Dried beans, corn, pennies, and so on
Stapler or tape

Put a handful of dried beans, corn, or pennies in a small aluminum tart pan. Place another tart pan over the top of the first and staple or tape the edges together.

Easter Egg Maracas

Small plastic Easter eggs
Pennies, dried beans, small rocks, popcorn kernels,
  beads, buttons, and so on
Glue gun
Empty egg carton

Gather a variety of items to fill the plastic Easter eggs. Try pennies, dried beans, small rocks, popcorn kernels, beads, buttons, and so on. Fill each egg with a different substance and securely glue the two pieces of the egg together. Store in an egg carton. Toddlers will enjoy taking the eggs in and out of the carton and shaking them to hear the different sounds they make.

For an older child, fill two eggs with each substance. Have him shake the eggs and match up the pairs by listening to the sounds they make.

Kazoo

Empty toilet paper roll
Thin paper (newspaper works well)
White glue
Hole punch
Scissors

Punch a hole in the side of the empty toilet paper roll as far from the end as the punch will reach. Cut a square of paper large enough to cover one end of the roll. Coat the edge of the roll with glue and press it firmly onto the square of paper. Leave the roll standing on the paper until the glue is completely dry. If you like, your child can decorate his kazoo with crayons, markers, or stickers.

To play the kazoo, show your child how to put his mouth against the open end of the kazoo and hum.

Jingle Bell Roller

Empty coffee can with lid
Jingle bells or jar lids

Put bells or metal jar lids inside the empty coffee can.
Securely glue or tape the plastic lid onto the coffee can. Your
child can help you decorate the outside of the coffee can. If
you like, try gluing a piece of contact paper sticky side out
around the can, then have your toddler stick on pictures cut
from magazines, pieces of gift-wrap, or whatever you have on
hand. Cover with another piece of contact paper. Your child
will have fun shaking the can or rolling it across the floor.

Dance and Fall Down

Music

Put on some music and dance around the room with your
child. When the music stops, everyone falls down. When the
music begins again, everyone gets up and dances some more.

Dancing with Scarves

Scarves are a versatile item to have on hand for toddlers.

Scarf (chiffon or other lightweight fabric)
Music

Choose a light, breezy scarf for your child to dance with. If the scarf is too long, tie a knot in the middle to form a handle. Encourage your child to wave his scarf in the air in time to the music.

Stop!

Face your child and hold his hands. Walk slowly in a circle and sing or recite this poem as you walk:

Round and round and round we go,
Round and round and round we go,
Round and round and round we go.
Round and round and STOP!

Freeze when you say "STOP!" Repeat the game as many times as your child wants to, changing directions and speeding up a little more each time.

Follow the Leader

Young children are such a bundle of energy. A short "exercise class" not only helps their large muscle development, but it can also be a sanity saver on a long, rainy day indoors. You'll feel better afterward, too!

Encourage your child to follow your lead as you exercise together. Try touching toes, running in place, swinging your arms, and stretching to the ceiling. Exercise to music, pass a ball back and forth, or twirl a long ribbon in the air. For a change, let your child be the leader and you follow his example.

Row, Row, Row Your Boat

Sit on the floor across from your child, legs spread far enough apart so that you can hold hands. Pull your child toward you, then lean forward and have your child lean back. Continue the rocking motion, forward and back, as you sing the familiar song "Row, Row, Row Your Boat" or other rocking rhymes.

Let's Pretend

This activity will give your child's large muscles a workout along with his imagination.

Give your child a series of instructions such as "Let's pretend you are a rabbit. Can you hop like a rabbit?" or "Let's pretend you are an elephant. Can you walk about like a big, heavy elephant?" Try other animals and include things such as plants growing in the ground, a flower opening on a summer day, or a balloon being filled with air.

Climbing Practice

Couch cushions or large pillows

Make a big, soft pile of couch cushions or large pillows on the floor. Your toddler will have fun climbing and rolling around on them. For older toddlers, stack the cushions up like stairs against the couch and let him practice climbing up and down.

Jingle Bell Bracelet

You might consider this most appropriate as a Christmas activity, but toddlers will enjoy jingling any time of year.

Jingle bells
Elastic cord
Scissors

Cut the elastic cord long enough to fit your child's wrist and add a few inches for tying. String three or four jingle bells onto the elastic and tie the ends together. Slip the bracelet onto your child's wrist or ankle, put some music on, and listen to the bells jingle as he dances or claps around the house.

Mirror Play

This activity will probably be best enjoyed by one-year-olds.

Large mirror

Stand or sit with your child in front of a large mirror. Ask your child what he sees and point out his head, arms, legs, feet, and so on. Encourage him to make movements and watch what happens to his reflection as he does. Put on some music and watch him move and dance in time to the beat. You may want to have your camera on hand in case he tries to kiss his reflection.

Toddler Trampoline

Crib mattress
Crib sheet
Pillows

Place a crib mattress on the floor, away from any dangerous edges or corners. Cover the mattress with a crib sheet and surround it with pillows for safety. Your child will enjoy jumping and bouncing on his toddler-sized trampoline.

Toddler Gymnastics

Simple gymnastics will not only burn up some of your toddler's seemingly endless energy, but it will also encourage his eye-body coordination, necessary for balance and depth perception.

Encourage your toddler in simple gymnastics such as tumbling, rolling, climbing, and sliding. If you like, put on some snappy music or play Follow the Leader. Show your child the basic movements, then take turns being the leader.

Dance Ribbon

Empty key chain or plastic shower curtain ring
Long lengths of brightly colored ribbon or plastic

Attach 3- or 4-foot lengths of brightly colored ribbon or plastic to an empty key chain or plastic shower curtain ring. Your child can wave the ribbon in the air as he runs or twirl it in time to the music as he dances.

CHAPTER 10
Arts and Crafts

"It would seem that something which means poverty, disorder, and violence every single day should be avoided entirely, but the desire to beget children is a natural urge."
—*Phyllis Diller*

Art and craft activities provide many valuable learning experiences for toddlers. Your child will begin to learn to think creatively, and activities such as drawing, painting, cutting, pasting, and playing with playdough and other craft materials will help develop fine motor and manipulative skills.

One important thing to keep in mind when doing any art or craft activity with a young child is that it's the process—not the product—that counts. By this I mean that activities which can provide so much benefit to a toddler can also lead to frustration and disappointment for both adult and child if the parent or caregiver comes to the activity with a final product in mind. The adult who has an expected outcome from a toddler art or craft activity will, out of necessity, do a lot of the work for the child. The child will end up with a nice picture or object, but any skills she may have learned from that experience will be lost or minimized. Even something as simple as using a glue stick is important for little ones, so resist the urge to grab it out of your child's hands and do it yourself if she's not doing it "right." We all know arts and crafts look better, go faster, and are neater if we do the work for our children, but if they're to gain any benefit at all from an activity, they have to do the work themselves.

Karen Miller, in her book *More Things to Do with Toddlers and Twos* (Telshare Publishing, 1990), lists five general principles for doing art with toddlers. While she is writing primarily for teachers of toddlers, these are great guidelines to keep in mind whether you're working with many toddlers or just one.

1. Don't tell your child what to make and don't expect her final product to be recognizable. Telling a two-year-old to make a mailbox or an Easter basket only sets her up for failure, as she cannot possibly do it herself. Instead, Miller says, "value the basic scribble." The most important thing for your child is the experience of freely exploring art and craft materials. Toddlers simply cannot control the materials well enough to make a representational drawing.

2. Focus on providing interesting materials. Toddlers are basically interested in cause and effect, whether they are playing with water, building with blocks, or working on an art project such as fingerpainting, pasting, or painting with a brush. Your goal in providing your toddler with art

experiences should be to expose her to as many different materials and processes as possible. Let her play with warm playdough one day, cold the next; mix paint thick one time, thin another; use wide and narrow paintbrushes as well as sponges, cotton swabs, and feathers for painting.

3. Let your child do the whole project. The activity only has value for the child if she does it herself. In making a collage with glue, the value for the child comes in spreading the glue on the page, noticing how it feels on her fingers, and so on. If you spread the glue on and then provide the items for your child to stick to the page, much of the value of the activity is lost.

4. Do art with one child at a time or with very small groups. Miller says that "with your undivided attention, the child can really concentrate on the material in front of her and enjoy seeing what she can do with it." If you do have other young children to care for, have other interesting things prepared for them to do while you're working one-on-one with your toddler, or allow them to stand around and watch if they want to. Older two- and three-year-olds may enjoy doing art in groups of three or four.

5. Allow children to repeat experiences. Sometimes we may feel that providing our children with a variety of experiences means never doing the same thing twice. What we're really doing, however, is not allowing our child to fully explore an

activity, meaning that the child cannot learn or develop as much. Allowing your toddler to repeat an activity several times gives her the opportunity to fully explore it and, as Miller states, "encourages the development of concentration and experimentation, both elements of creativity."

Don't forget to display the artwork your child has created. Post it on walls, doors, and of course the refrigerator. Use it to create a custom tablecloth: cover your table with a plain dark tablecloth, arrange your child's artwork on it, then cover with a clear vinyl tablecloth. Use your child's artwork as a gift or gift-wrap when possible. If you like, create a portfolio for your child. Use a three-ring binder and plastic page protectors to save some of your child's earliest or most outstanding creations. (Be sure to date or write your child's age on each work of art.) For extralarge or three-dimensional projects, take a photo or two and put those in the binder.

The activities in this chapter will help you provide your toddler with a variety of art and craft experiences. These experiences should be fun for you and your child, so don't undertake painting or other messy projects when you're tired, rushed, or otherwise unable to devote yourself fully to what your toddler is doing. With the right attitude, you and your toddler will have a wonderful time creating, exploring, and discovering the world of art.

Scribbling and Drawing

When I first became a mother, I purchased a very good book on things to do with babies. It stated that children should start to scribble between nine and twelve months of age, and it even outlined the procedure to follow: seat your child comfortably, then give her some paper and a big fat crayon. Show her how to make marks on the page, then watch her go.

I was horrified to realize that time had gotten away from me! My daughter, already past her first birthday, had not yet had her first experience with crayons and paper. After a quick run to the store, I optimistically seated her in her highchair, taped down a piece of blank paper, showed her how to hold the crayon, and let her go to it. You can imagine my dismay when she began eating the crayon and tearing the paper! She wasn't lagging behind developmentally, as I initially feared; she just wasn't ready for the whole scribbling experience.

When ready for it, most toddlers will find scribbling a lot of fun. It allows them to experiment with cause and effect while developing small muscles and hand-eye coordination. Cynthia Catlin, in her book *Toddlers Together: The Complete Planning Guide for a Toddler Curriculum* (Gryphon House, 1994), says, "Scribbling is the precursor to writing, just as babbling is to talking. A better term for scribbling would be M.I.M.s, for these are the Most Important Marks a toddler can make."

Provide your toddler with a variety of drawing tools and materials: crayons, markers, pens, pencil crayons, and chalk. For drawing paper, use construction paper, newsprint, fine sandpaper, or cut-open grocery bags. Remember to include three-dimensional surfaces such as boxes and rocks.

If replacing caps on markers is a problem, make this simple marker holder: Mix plaster of Paris in a small plastic container that is at least as deep as a marker top. Set the marker tops in the wet plaster with the open end up. Be sure that the plaster does not cover the open end of the marker top. When the plaster dries, press the markers into their tops that have dried into the plaster. Remind your child to stand the markers back in the marker holder when she has finished using them.

Rainbow Crayons

This idea appears in *The Preschooler's Busy Book,* but it's worth repeating here. These crayons are beautiful and easy for little hands to hold!

Broken crayon pieces
Clean, empty tin cans
Pot of hot water
Empty plastic film canisters

This is a great way to use broken crayons. Remove any paper from the crayons and sort them by color. Place the pieces, one color at a time, in the empty tin cans. Set the tin cans in a pot of very hot or boiling water until the crayons have melted. Pour a small amount (approximately a quarter inch) into each film canister. When the wax hardens, add a second color in the same way. When you're done, you will have a crayon rainbow of layered colors.

Cylinder Pictures

Paper
Markers or crayons
Tape

Have your child draw on a rectangular piece of paper. When she's done, roll the paper into a cylinder and tape the ends together. Set it on a shelf or mantle for all to admire.

Marker Drawing

Here's a good way to get more use out of dried-up markers.

Dried-up markers
Water
Paper

Let your child dip dried-up markers in water and use them like watercolors on paper. When the tips turn white, you can throw the markers away or dip them in paint and use them as paintbrushes.

Foot Tracing

Drawing paper
Crayons, markers, or paints

Have your child stand on a piece of paper while you trace
around her feet with a pen or crayon. Then trace your own
feet and compare sizes. Color the feet with crayons, markers,
or paints. Older children may want to use crayons, markers,
or paint to add nail polish and funny rings to the toes.

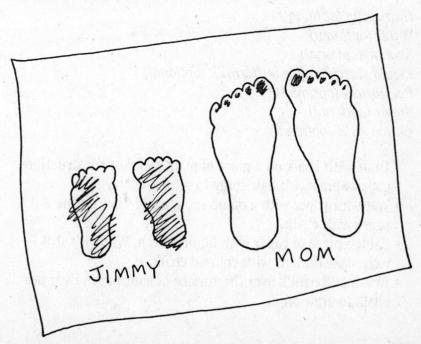

Chalk Fun

There was a time that chalk was just for chalkboards and side-walks. Now inexpensive chalk is available in a variety of colors and thicknesses, and you can use it creatively in many different art endeavors. The following ideas will help you use chalk in ways you may not have considered before.

Chalk
Paper
Hair spray (optional)
Water (optional)
Sponge (optional)
Liquid starch and/or buttermilk (optional)
Paintbrush (optional)
Sugar (optional)
Cotton balls (optional)

- Draw with chalk on a piece of plain paper or construction paper. Spray with hair spray to set the chalk.
- Wet your paper with a damp sponge and draw on the wet paper with chalk.
- Paint a piece of paper with liquid starch. While it's still wet, make designs with colored chalk.
- Brush buttermilk over the surface of your paper, then use chalk to draw on it.

- Place a piece of paper on a textured surface (such as a sidewalk) or over a greeting card with a raised design. Rub a piece of chalk sideways over the paper to make a chalk rubbing of the texture or design.
- Draw on a window with wet chalk. It will easily wash away when you're done.
- Soak chalk in a mixture of 1 cup water and ⅓ cup sugar for 5 to 10 minutes. Draw with the wet chalk on a piece of paper. Use a cotton ball to smudge the chalk marks on the paper.

Paper Towel Drawing

A quick and easy activity for even the youngest toddlers.

Paper towel or coffee filters
Markers

Set your toddler in her highchair and give her a couple of markers and a piece of paper towel or coffee filter. The absorbency of the paper towel will make the colors blur as she makes marks on it.

Toddler Mural

Toddlers love to color and will usually color on anything and everything if you let them. Try this idea if you have a runaway artist in your home.

Large sheet of drawing paper
Art easel
Fat crayons
Yarn
Scissors

Tape a large sheet of drawing paper to the easel. Cut several pieces of yarn about 2 feet in length. Cut a small notch at one end of each crayon and wrap and tie a length of yarn around it. Tie the other end of the yarn to the top of the easel. (Be sure to cut the yarn long enough to reach the paper, but not so long that it poses a choking hazard.) Now your toddler can scribble any time she wants without waiting for you to set out the crayons and paper.

If you don't have an art easel but do have an empty wall in the basement or playroom, use that instead. Tape a large sheet of paper to the wall. Above the paper, hammer in a few nails and attach the yarn and crayons to the nails.

Painting

A child's love for paint begins at an early age and lasts for many years, if not a lifetime. A clean sheet of paper before her, pots of paint in vivid colors, big paintbrushes to wield as she wills—what could make a toddler happier?

If proper preparations have been made, this art experience can be enjoyed by the parent or caregiver, too. Before you begin a painting session with your toddler, consider the following guidelines:

- Don't undertake a painting session with your toddler when you're tired, rushed, or otherwise unable to devote yourself fully to what your child is doing.
- Cover up the work space appropriately. I cover the kitchen table with a big old sheet that I throw in the wash when the painting session is over.
- If you don't have a painter's smock or big old T-shirt to cover your child, dress her in old clothes that you can afford to set aside as painting clothes. (Even washable paints may not wash out completely.)
- Add a little dish detergent or water and soap flakes to the paint. It makes cleanup easier.

The best kind of paint for young children is poster paint, also known as tempera paint, which you can buy at any art store in premixed liquid form or as a powder that must be mixed with water. You can also make your own poster paint using the recipes in Appendix A. Children rarely need more than three colors: red, blue, and yellow. Teach your child how to mix these colors to create others. Tempera blocks are also available. They're practical because they don't have to be diluted and they can't be spilled, making cleanup easier. In addition, tempera blocks are economical and last a long time.

However, your child will probably not find them as fun as slick liquid paints. Empty baby-food jars work well as paint jars. You can use a sponge to prevent the jar from tipping and soak up any drips. Simply cut a hole in the sponge the size of the jar and fit the jar into the sponge. You can also make a simple toddler-size paint palette by gluing plastic milk lids to a piece of heavy cardboard. Pour a small amount of paint into each lid. For a more permanent palette, nail several baby-food jar lids to a block of wood.

Paper can be purchased from an art supply store, but consider some of the following alternatives. Newsprint is a wonderful paper for painting, and roll ends can be purchased cheaply from a newspaper publisher. Visit your local printer and ask if you can leave an empty box for a week or two. She may agree to fill it with all kinds of wonderful paper that would otherwise be discarded. Also try fine sandpaper as an alternative art paper for a wonderful effect. For fingerpainting, use the shiny side of freezer paper that can be purchased at the grocery store. It's much cheaper than special finger-paint paper and works just as well.

If you have an old wall you don't care too much about, cover it with a large piece of contact paper. You can tape the painting paper directly to the contact paper, and it will wipe up easily. The contact paper will likely damage the wall if you try to remove it, so be careful where you put it.

A tabletop easel can be made by removing one side of a cardboard box and taping the remaining three sides to form a triangle shape. Tape one side to the table and attach a piece of paper to one of the other sides. Use it for painting or drawing. Here are a few more tips to keep in mind when working with paint:

- Water and soap flakes or detergent added to paint make it easier to wash out.
- Liquid detergent added to paint will help prevent cracking.
- Liquid starch will make paint thicker.
- Condensed milk will give paint a glossier finish.
- Powdered alum can be used as a preservative.
- Salt, crushed eggshells, and coffee grounds give paint an interesting texture.
- Baby powder mixed with tempera paint will extend the paint and add a nice smell.
- Plastic cafeteria trays are ideal for toddlers to paint on, with or without paper.
- String up a line in the laundry room or kitchen that can be used to hang paintings to dry. Wet artwork can be attached to the line with clothespins. When dry, be sure to display your child's paintings prominently. Think of creative uses for some of her work: Many painting projects make wonderful gift-wrap or greeting cards.

Straw Painting

If your child has mastered the skill of blowing, she may enjoy this activity. If not, she will still enjoy using the straw as a paintbrush.

Tempera paint
Paper
Drinking straw

Drop a bit of thin paint on a piece of paper. Give your child a straw and have her blow the paint around. If you like, add a second and third color. You can also try different types of paper for different effects.

Paint with Water

Black marker
Paper towel
Paintbrush
Water

Draw a picture or shape with a thick black marker on a piece of paper towel. Show your child how to brush water over the marker lines and watch how the colors seep out.

Dry Painting

For a painting activity, this is pretty clean and requires little preparation.

Cotton balls
Clothespins (spring-type)
Powdered tempera paint
Paper
Hair spray

Clip a cotton ball onto the end of a spring-type clothespin. Sprinkle a few colors of powdered tempera paint onto a piece of paper. Show your toddler how to use the cotton ball to spread the paint around the paper. When the painting is done, spray it with hair spray to set the paint. It will make a nice greeting card.

Crumple Painting

Here's another easy way for your young child to make wrapping paper.

Liquid tempera paint or soap paint
  (see Frosty Soap Painting, page 254)
Newspaper
Heavy plain paper

Crumple up some newspaper into a ball and dip it in liquid tempera or soap paint. Press the newspaper ball lightly all over the heavy plain paper. Use two or three different colors if you like. Let dry.

Marker Painting

Dried-up markers
Tempera paint
Paper

Let your child use dried-up markers in place of a paintbrush. Dip them in liquid tempera paint and use to write or draw on paper.

Food-Coloring Painting

Food coloring
Water
Paintbrush
Paper towel or coffee filter

Add food coloring to water, enough to achieve the color you want. Brush the food coloring and water mixture onto a piece of paper towel or coffee filter. Use several colors. When the paper towel is soaked, remove and let dry, then mount on construction paper to display.

Magic Painting

"Paint with water" book
Ice cube or ice Popsicle

For a variation on painting with a brush and water, use an ice cube or ice Popsicle to paint on pages from a "paint with water" book. Or place a "paint with water" page in a baking pan, add an ice cube, and let your child move the pan around and watch the picture come to life.

Sheet Painting

Spray bottle
Water
Liquid tempera paint
Old sheet

Fill a spray bottle half with water and half with tempera paint. For some creative outdoor fun, hang an old sheet on a fence or clothesline and have your child spray-paint it.

Fly Swatter Painting

This is definitely an outdoor activity. If it's just "something to do," then one color of paint is enough. For a nicer-looking painting, try using two or three colors of paint, one after the other.

Fly swatter
Paint
Baking pan or cookie sheet
Large sheets of paper

Put up large sheets of paper outside, either by taping them to a fence or clipping them to a clothesline. Pour paint into the baking pan or cookie sheet. Show your child how to dip the fly swatter into the paint and slap it onto the paper.

Paint Popsicles

Please supervise this activity carefully and use it only with children who are not likely to lick these Popsicles. For safer variations for really young children, try Ice Popsicle Painting or Ice Cube Painting.

Liquid tempera paint
Water
Popsicle mold
Paper

Mix one part tempera paint with one part water and pour into a Popsicle mold. Insert sticks and place in the freezer until frozen. Remove paint Popsicles from the freezer about 10 minutes before you want to use them. Give your child the paint Popsicle and a large piece of paper and let her paint away.

Ice Popsicle Painting

This variation of Paint Popsicles is more suited to younger children. If you think your child may lick the ice Popsicle after it's been used to paint, try substituting Kool-Aid drink mix or Jell-O powder for powdered paint.

Water
Popsicle mold
Powdered tempera paint
Paper

Freeze water in a Popsicle mold to make ice Popsicles. Remove from the freezer a few minutes before using to allow the ice to melt a little. Sprinkle a little tempera powder on a piece of paper. Your child can paint by rubbing the ice Popsicle over the paint on the paper.

Squeeze Painting

Flour
Salt
Water
Food coloring or liquid tempera paint (optional)
Squeeze bottles or small spoons
Paper

Mix equal parts of flour, salt, and water. If working on colored paper, leave the paint white; if using white paper, add a few drops of food coloring or liquid tempera to the paint. Pour the paint into squeeze bottles or use a small spoon to dribble the paint onto the paper. Let dry, and admire the sparkly results.

Ice Cube Painting

Ice cubes
Paper
Powdered tempera paint
Flat box (the kind a 24-pack of soda
  comes in) or large baking pan

Place a sheet of paper in the box or baking pan. Sprinkle a
little tempera powder on the paper. Place the ice cube in the
box and let your child rotate the box around to make a pretty
painting. If you like, substitute Kool-Aid drink mix or Jell-O
powder for the powdered tempera paint.

Rainbow Painting

The wet paper really makes the colors flow and blend for a beautiful effect.

Paper
Water
Wide paintbrush or sponge
Paints or washable markers

Paint a sheet of paper with water using a wide paintbrush or a wet sponge. Your child can paint lines of color across the page with paints, or draw on it with washable markers.

Cling Wrap Painting

White paper
Paint
Spoons
Plastic cling wrap

Using a spoon, dribble paint onto the paper. Use several different colors. Place a sheet of plastic cling wrap over the paint (make sure the cling wrap covers the whole surface). Use your hands to smooth the cling wrap over the paper, then carefully peel it off. Allow the painting to dry.

Painted Place Mat

Rubber cement
White construction paper
Tempera paint
Paintbrushes
Clear contact paper

Dribble rubber cement randomly or in a design over a sheet of white construction paper. Allow to dry for about 30 minutes, then paint over the rubber cement using tempera paint in one or more colors. Allow the paint to dry, then peel the rubber cement off the construction paper to see the design that is left. Cover both sides of the painting with clear contact paper to make it into a place mat.

Feather Painting

For this activity you can use colorful feathers from the craft store or bird feathers you find outside.

Feathers
Glue
Tempera paint
Paper

Mix a little bit of glue with the tempera paint. Use feathers to brush the paint onto the paper. If you like, leave a few feathers on the painting to make a feather collage. (When the paint dries, the glue mixed with it will make the feathers stick.) You can also try this with pine branches, leaves, flowers, or other natural objects that may be good for painting.

Salad Spinner Art

This is a good activity for older toddlers. You may want to donate your salad spinner to the craft box after you do this activity.

Salad spinner
Paper plate
Paint

Remove the plastic insert from the salad spinner and place a small paper plate in the bottom. Replace the insert on top of the paper plate. Dribble a little paint into the spinner, put the lid on, and spin. If you like, add another color or two and spin some more for a nice effect.

Rock Painting

Golf balls or Ping-Pong balls also work well for this activity.

Shoebox with lid or diaper-wipe container
Paper
Scissors
Tempera paint
Rock

Cut a piece of plain paper or construction paper to fit the bottom of the shoebox or diaper-wipe container. Pour a small amount of paint into a dish and dip a rock in the paint. Place the rock into the shoebox or container and shut the lid. Shake the box up and down and from side to side. Open the lid and look at the design the rock has made. Dip the rock in another color of paint and repeat the shaking procedure until your child tires of it.

Paint Dancing

Large sheet or piece of fabric
Baking pan or tray for paint
Liquid tempera paint
Warm, soapy water
Towels
Music

Tape a large sheet or piece of fabric securely to the floor or lay it on the ground outside. Fill a baking pan or tray with paint. Add a little liquid soap or dish detergent to make cleanup easier. Put on some music and roll up your child's pant legs, or dress her in only a diaper or shorts. Have her step into the tray of paint, then onto the bedsheet. Then have her dance to the music! Have a pan of warm, soapy water and a towel on hand for when she tires of this activity (or if she refuses to stay on the sheet).

Paint Pen

This idea from *The Preschooler's Busy Book* is such a great activity for toddlers that I thought it worth repeating.

Empty roll-on deodorant bottle or shoe polish bottle
Liquid tempera paint

To make a giant paint pen for your child, pry the top off a roll-on deodorant or shoe polish bottle. Fill it with tempera paint (mixed fairly thickly) and snap the top back on the bottle. Your child can use this for a quick and easy painting activity.

For an easy alternative, use bingo dabbers already filled with ink. The disadvantage of this technique is that the ink isn't washable and doesn't flow as well as paint.

String Painting

Yarn or string
Scissors
Tape
Popsicle sticks
Liquid tempera paint
Paper

Tape 5-inch pieces of yarn or string to the end of a Popsicle stick. Using the stick as a handle, dip the string into liquid tempera paint and drag it across and around the paper.

Frosty Soap Painting

1 cup powdered laundry soap
½ cup cold water
Electric mixer or wire whisk
Food coloring (optional)
Paintbrushes
Heavy paper or cardboard

Beat or whisk cold water and laundry soap together until stiff. Add food coloring or leave white if using colored paper. Paint with a brush or use as fingerpaint on heavy paper or cardboard. Let dry flat.

Fingerpainting

Fingerpaints
Fingerpaint or butcher paper

Fingerpainting is a wonderfully messy adventure that every child should experience after the age of two—or younger, if you can stand it! Unfortunately, it can be frustrating for parents, as the amount of work required to set up and clean up never seems to merit the 5 minutes (or less) most children will spend at this activity. That said, be prepared for a great big mess, and make sure your child wears an art smock.

Wet the paper first to allow the paint to slide better. Drop a blob of paint on the paper and let your child go at it. You can buy commercial fingerpaint or make your own using the recipes in Appendix A.

For variety, use fingerpaint that has been chilled or warmed. Add salt or sand for texture. Thick fingerpaint or fingerpaint mixed with salt or sand can also be pushed around the paper with a Popsicle stick or spoon.

If you like, have your child fingerpaint on a tabletop or highchair tray, then press a piece of paper over the paint to make a print to save. Plastic cafeteria trays are great surfaces for fingerpainting, or try painting on a window or mirror. (Adding a little liquid detergent to the paint makes cleanup easier.)

Bathtub Fingerpainting

This is a great idea for the youngest artists in your house.

Fingerpaint
Newsprint

Dress your one-year-old in a diaper and an old shirt. Place her in a dry bathtub with a blob of fingerpaint and watch the results! When her work is complete, lay a piece of newsprint over it, press gently, and lift for a copy of her masterpiece.

Shaving Cream Fingerpaint

I wouldn't advise this activity for children with sensitive skin or those prone to licking their fingers! If you like, substitute whipped cream or instant pudding.

Shaving cream
Food coloring or tempera paint

Squirt some shaving cream onto a tabletop, highchair tray, or piece of paper. Add a few drops of food coloring or sprinkle a bit of powdered tempera paint for instant fingerpaint fun.

Food-Coloring Fingerpaint

Food coloring will stain your child's fingers for a day or two, so avoid this activity if your child needs to look her best shortly after your fun.

Corn syrup
Brush
Food coloring
Heavy paper or posterboard

Spread corn syrup over a piece of heavy paper or posterboard. Drop a few drops of food coloring in various colors onto the paper. Your child will have fun spreading the colors around with her fingers. When the picture dries, it will be shiny and beautiful!

Printmaking

Printmaking involves making an impression of an object on paper or another surface. The object to be printed can be covered in paint with a brush or roller, dipped in paint, or pressed on a print pad.

A print pad can be made by wadding up newspaper and soaking it in liquid tempera paint. Or you can place a thin sponge in a shallow tray or small bowl and cover with several tablespoons of paint. For some printmaking, an ink pad can be used. To cushion a print, place a newspaper under the paper on which the impression is to be made.

Many different types of paper can be used for printing: newsprint, construction paper, and brown paper bags are some of the cheaper options. As with many of the painting projects in this chapter, you can use these printing activities to create some great environmentally friendly gift-wrap.

Very young toddlers are not likely to understand the print-making process. They tend to use the object to be printed more like a sponge or paintbrush, and usually end up just pushing it around the paper. Older two- and three-year-olds will enjoy making prints. Encourage them to press the object gently into the paint and then onto the paper to make a successful print.

Bubble Wrap Printing

Bubble wrap packing material
Tape
Liquid tempera paint (several different colors)
Paintbrush
Paper

Tape the bubble wrap to the table or surface you will be painting on. Have your child paint on the bubble wrap, then press a piece of paper on it to get an interesting print.

Cork Printing

Wine bottle corks
Liquid tempera paint in a shallow pan
Paper

Grasp the cork at one end and hold it upright. Press the cork into the paint then onto a piece of paper or newsprint. If you like, use tempera paint in several different colors.

Block Printing

Small blocks of wood
Rickrack
Glue
Liquid tempera paint in a shallow pan
Paper

Glue rickrack to the end of a block of wood. Press the block into the paint, then onto paper to make a zigzag design. Move the block around in different directions and add different colors of paint if you like.

For an alternate activity, wrap string around a block or glue an object such as a key or small plastic ring to the end of the block to make an interesting print.

Muffin Tin Printing

Muffin tin
Liquid tempera paint (several different colors)
Paintbrush
Paper

Place a muffin tin upside down on a covered surface. Have your child paint the bottoms of the muffin cups. When she's done, place a piece of paper over the muffin tin and press to make a print of her work.

Glue Printing

Various objects to print
White glue
Glitter
Paper

Instead of using paint or an ink pad for printing, try using glue and glitter. Press objects (fruits and vegetables cut in half, sponges cut into shapes, string wrapped around a block of wood, and so on) into glue, then onto paper. Sprinkle the paper with glitter or colored sand and let dry. Large pieces of newsprint covered with glitter make nice gift-wrap.

Berry Basket Printing

Pint-size berry baskets
Liquid tempera paint
Flat containers for paint
Paper

Pour a small amount of paint into flat containers big enough to fit the berry basket. Place the berry basket bottom-side-down into the paint. Make prints on the paper by pressing the paint-covered bottom of the basket on the paper. Change colors if you like.

Toy Car Printing

Toy cars or trucks with wide wheels
Liquid tempera paint
Paper

Pour a small amount of paint in a container big enough to dip the wheels of the toy car or truck in. Place the car or truck into the paint and roll it back and forth a time or two so that the wheels are covered with paint. Roll the car or truck across the paper to make tire tracks.

Spool Printing

Print pad or liquid tempera paint
Empty thread spools
Paper

Press empty thread spools onto a print pad or dip them in liquid tempera paint. Press onto paper to make the shape of a tire.

Duplo Printing

Duplo pieces in different sizes
Liquid tempera paint
Paper

Pour a small amount of paint into a container big enough to dip the Duplo in. Place the Duplo upside down in the paint. Press the paint-covered Duplo onto the paper to make a print. Use both sides of the Duplo and different colors of paint for an interesting design.

Cardboard Printing

Corrugated cardboard
Tape or rubber band
Liquid tempera paint
Construction paper

Cut a strip of corrugated cardboard about 6 inches by 10 inches. Make sure the corrugated ridges run parallel to the 6-inch sides. Place the cardboard on the table in front of you, smooth side up. Starting with a 6-inch side, roll up the cardboard tightly. Make sure the corrugated ridges end up on the outside of the roll. Secure the roll with tape or a rubber band. Dip the end of the cardboard roll into the paint and press onto paper to make a flowerlike print.

Sponge Printing

Sponge
Chalk
Water
Paper

Soak a sponge in water and squeeze to release the excess. Use a piece of chalk to draw on the wet sponge. Press the wet sponge onto a piece of white or colored construction paper to create a print. If you like, use chalk in various colors and a variety of sponges in different shapes and sizes.

Tearing, Gluing, and Sticking

Toddlers, paper, and glue are a great combination. What child hasn't discovered early in life the special joy of scrunching and tearing paper? Keep a stack of old magazines on hand for tearing. (Most toddlers and young preschoolers can't yet handle a pair of scissors, so avoid frustration and tear everything.)

Gluing is great fun, too. Toddlers enjoy the glue itself as much as whatever it is you're having them make. Vary the type of glue your child uses: a glue stick, glue in a bottle, or spreadable paste. Pour a small amount of white glue into a baby-food jar lid and add a drop or two of food coloring. Use a small paintbrush or cotton swab to spread the glue around.

Provide your child with lots of interesting things to stick: greeting cards, fabric scraps, and paper scraps (tissue, wrapping, and construction paper). You can also use pasta, yarn, cotton balls, and bits of ribbon. Outdoor walks can yield a wonderful supply of new materials including leaves, pine needles, flower petals, and so on. You should also vary the surface onto which your child sticks things: paper plates, cardboard pieces, egg cartons, empty tissue boxes, and paper of all shapes, sizes, and colors.

The most important thing about tearing, gluing, and sticking is that your child should do the whole project by herself. Varying the materials used will keep the same basic activity interesting for both you and your child.

Paper Bag Faces

Some toddlers may lose interest in this activity once the paper bag is stuffed. That's okay, because the real value of this activity for the toddler is in the tearing of paper.

Newspaper or old magazines for tearing
Paper bag
Rubber band
Crayon, marker, or paint

Tear up old newspapers or magazines. Crumple up the pieces and stuff them in a paper bag. When the bag is full, seal the end with a rubber band. Then draw or paint a big happy face on the paper bag. This item will work well as a large, light-weight object for your toddler to lift, carry, or throw.

Popcorn Picture

Popped popcorn
Glue stick or white glue
Construction paper
Brown paper bag (optional)
Tempera paint powder (optional)

Rub the glue stick on a piece of construction paper or spread white glue with a brush. Stick popped popcorn onto the construction paper to make a collage. For a winter scene, use plain white popcorn. For spring blossoms, shake the popcorn in a brown paper bag with powdered tempera paint, then glue the popcorn onto a flower shape cut from construction paper. For variety, try using Cheerios or puffed rice cereal instead.

Gift-Wrap Collage

Gift-wrap
Tissue paper
Scissors
Construction paper
Glue stick
Clear contact paper (optional)

Save pieces of gift-wrap and tissue paper from birthdays and other gift-giving occasions. Cut or tear the paper into interesting shapes and save in a box or Ziploc freezer bag.

Show your child how to rub the glue stick onto a piece of paper, and then how to press a colorful paper shape onto the glued area. If you like, use a piece of clear contact paper taped to the table sticky side up in place of the construction paper and glue.

Tissue Paper Collage

Aluminum foil
Colored tissue paper
Scissors (optional)
Baby oil
Paintbrush

Tear off a piece of aluminum foil about the size of a piece of paper. Cut or tear the tissue paper into small pieces. Squeeze a few drops of baby oil onto the tin foil and spread around with a paintbrush. Show your child how the tissue paper will stick to the foil wherever the baby oil is, but can be easily removed. Use different colors of tissue paper to make a collage.

Froot Loop Sand

Froot Loops cereal
Food processor or rolling pin
Construction paper
Glue stick

Make Froot Loop Sand by crushing Froot Loops cereal in a
food processor or with a rolling pin. Rub the glue stick onto a
piece of construction paper, then sprinkle the Froot Loop
sand onto it. If your child dumps the sand onto the picture all
at once, that's okay; just tip the picture onto another piece of
paper and the excess will slide off. For variety, try using a
clean, empty spice container to shake the Froot Loop sand
onto the glue.

Salt Pictures

Salt (or clean sand)
Tempera paint powder
Empty salt and pepper shakers or spice containers
Paper
Glue
Paintbrush or spoon

Mix salt or sand with tempera paint powder in small shaker-type containers, one for each color. Brush glue onto paper with a small brush or dribble it on with a spoon. (Little ones may enjoy smearing the glue around with their fingers.) Sprinkle the salt/paint mixture over the paper. When the glue is dry, tip off the excess salt and hang to display.

Wax Paper Art

A safe and easy alternative to grated crayons and an iron.

Glue
Liquid tempera paint or food coloring
Paintbrush
Wax paper
Colorful leaves

Mix glue with tempera paint or food coloring to achieve a bright color (or use colored glue thinned with a little water). Using a brush, paint glue onto two pieces of wax paper of the same size (the paper should be well coated with glue). Stick colorful leaves onto the glue on one piece of paper, then cover with the other sheet. Press together to stick, then hang in a window.

Glitter Shapes

Construction paper
Scissors
Glue stick
Glitter or confetti
Small shoebox with lid
Rubber bands

Cut shapes out of construction paper. Use basic geometric shapes such as circles, squares, triangles, or rectangles, or seasonal shapes such as hearts, pumpkins, candy canes, and so on. Rub the glue stick on one or both sides of the shapes. Put the glue-covered shape into the shoebox along with confetti or glitter. Place the lid on the shoebox and secure with a couple of rubber bands. Shake the box to cover the shape with glitter or confetti. Remove the shape from the box and allow to dry.

Tape Collage

Toddlers and tape go together in a special way.

Tape (masking, cellophane, colored, and so on)
Small can or plastic container
Construction paper

Use an upside-down can (such as a tuna can) or plastic container as a tape holder for your child. Cut or tear off various lengths of tape and place them around the edges of the tape holder so that your child can pull them off easily. Use as many different types and colors of tape as you can. Give your child a piece of construction paper and show her how to pull a piece of tape off the tape holder and stick it onto the paper to make a collage.

Spaghetti Mobiles

If your child is likely to eat the glue-covered noodles, substitute corn syrup thinned with a little water for the glue. Many toddlers will enjoy just playing with warm spaghetti noodles on a highchair tray or tabletop.

White glue (or corn syrup)
Food coloring in 2–3 different colors
Containers for glue
Cooked spaghetti noodles
Styrofoam meat tray
Yarn or ribbon

Decide how many colors of glue you want to make, and pour the glue into that many containers. Add a few drops of food coloring to each glue container, using a different color for each container. Show your child how to dip the spaghetti, one piece at a time, into the colored glue, and lay it on the Styrofoam meat tray. Repeat, using different colors of glue, until your child tires of this activity. Let the noodles dry, then remove from the meat tray, tie on a piece of yarn or ribbon, and hang from the ceiling as a mobile.

Pathfinding

This is an excellent activity for developing small muscles. Using scissors is too tough for young toddlers, but older two- or three-year-olds can definitely give it a try. If paper is too difficult to cut, try playdough instead.

Pen or pencil
Paper
Child's scissors

Draw an easy-to-cut pattern (using two lines to form a path) on a plain piece of paper. Paths could follow a variety of shapes: zigzags, S-shapes, straight lines, and so on. Have your child cut right down the center of the path without straying. If you like, keep your child's cutting exercises in a special folder that you can add to each day.

Crafts and Other Fun Things to Make

Craft projects will challenge your child's imagination and artistic ability, and they will facilitate the development of fine motor skills. They may also fill in the long hours of a rainy day, keeping your child stimulated and happy.

Don't forget that for toddlers, it's the process that counts—not the product. Don't be discouraged if your child won't do it the "right" way. Perhaps she's still too young to be working on these crafts, or perhaps you need to let her freely explore the craft materials she's using and create a masterpiece of her own.

Toddler Collage

You may do this activity in one sitting or spread it out over a couple of days by adding interesting objects as you find them.

Clear contact paper
Scissors
Variety of objects to stick
Construction paper (optional)

Cut two pieces of clear contact paper about the size of a piece of paper, or larger if you like. Remove the backing from one piece of contact paper and lay it on a flat surface such as a table or highchair tray, sticky side up. Tape the corners to the table or highchair tray so that the contact paper won't move around. (If you're planning on working on the collage over a couple of days, tape the contact paper to a cardboard box that can be moved out of the way when you're not working on it.)

Provide a variety of interesting objects for your toddler to stick to the contact paper. Try scraps of tissue or wrapping paper, bits of colorful yarn or ribbon, small pieces of pasta, cotton balls, or leaves or flower petals. When her collage is done, cover it with the other piece of contact paper, or use a piece of construction paper instead. Hang in a window or on the wall for all to admire, or use as a unique place mat.

Sticker Art

Stickers come in handy for making quick crafts and matching games, decorating cards and gifts, making charts, and so on. Children of all ages love stickers. Now is the time to begin a collection, if you haven't started one already.

Stickers
Paper
Paper plate (optional)
Small soda bottle or plastic vitamin bottle (optional)

Show your child how to peel the sticker off the backing and press it to a piece of paper. To make a wall hanging, press stickers to a paper plate. Make a vase by decorating a small soda or plastic vitamin bottle. You can also color on plain white labels to make your own stickers.

Artwork Display

Here's a way to display your child's artwork on the refrigerator without having to cover it up with magnets to keep it there!

Wooden ruler (12-, 18-, or 24-inch)
Magnet strip (same length as ruler)
Glue gun
Clothespins, spring-type (at least 2)

Glue the magnetic strip to the back of the wooden ruler. Glue spring-type clothespins to the front of the ruler so that the pins open downward. Use two clothespins for a 12-inch ruler, placing one at each end. You may want to use three or four clothespins for a longer ruler. Write your child's name with marker or glitter on the front of the ruler, or let your child decorate the ruler and clothespins with paint, glitter, pasta, and so on. When dry, place the ruler on the refrigerator and clip your child's artwork with the clothespins.

Fishy Beanbag

Your child will have as much fun helping you make this easy beanbag as she will playing with it.

Tube sock
Dried beans
Yarn
Marker
Glue
Felt scraps (optional)

Fill a child-size tube sock about three-quarters full with dried beans. Tie tightly with yarn to make a tail. Push in the toe of the sock to form the mouth, and insert glue to hold the shape. Use a marker to draw eyes and gills, or you can cut eyes, gills, and fins from scraps of felt and glue them to the sock. Use the fishy beanbag to play catch, or try to throw it in an empty laundry basket.

Footprint T-shirt

This makes a great gift for moms, dads, and grandparents.

Fabric paint
Paintbrush
White T-shirt

Paint your child's feet and press them onto a white T-shirt. You can paint them different colors and press them randomly over the shirt, or use one color and make a trail of footprints up the front and down the back of the shirt. Personalize the T-shirt even more with an iron-on photograph or a special message written in fabric paint.

Fishy Necklace

This makes a great seasonal activity, too. Instead of fish, cut holiday shapes such as hearts or shamrocks.

Uncooked tube-shaped pasta, dyed or painted in bright colors
Construction paper
Hole punch
Shoelace (18 inches or longer)
Scissors

Cut 3- to 4-inch-long fish shapes from various colors of construction paper; punch a hole for an eye in each fish. Show your child how to string the painted or dyed pasta alternately with the fish shapes onto the shoelace; tie the ends together to make a necklace. (Instead of using tube-shaped pasta, you can use straws cut into 1½-inch lengths, but these will be more difficult for toddlers to string.)

Bookmark

Here's another great gift idea for grandparents. You can also use these bookmarks as unique thank-you cards for gifts your child has received.

Pencil for tracing
Paper
Scissors
Crayons, markers, stickers, and glitter for decorating
Clear contact paper

Place your child's hand and arm on a piece of paper and trace around it. Cut the tracing out of paper and have your child decorate it with crayons, markers, stickers, glitter, and so on. Be sure to write your child's name and age or date on the back. Cover with clear contact paper and use for a bookmark.

Bedtime Buddy

Roll of drawing paper
Pen or marker
Old sheet
Scissors
Sewing machine or needle and thread
Cotton batting
Fabric paint

Have your child lie down on a large piece of drawing paper and trace around her body. Cut out the outline and use it as a pattern to cut two body outlines out of an old sheet. Sew them together around the edges, right sides in, leaving enough of the edges unsewn to turn the right sides out. Turn, stuff with cotton batting, and sew the hole closed. Decorate with fabric paint and dress in your child's clothes.

CHAPTER 11

Birthday and Holiday Activities

"Of course, parents don't have children because they want to be martyrs, or at least they shouldn't. They have them because they love children and want some of their very own. They also love children because they remember being loved so much by their parents in their childhood. Taking care of their children, seeing them grow and develop into fine people, gives most parents despite the hard work their greatest satisfaction in life."
—*Dr. Benjamin Spock*

Holiday celebrations provide an important break from the day-to-day routine for children and adults. Whether you're preparing for a major celebration such as Christmas or Hanukkah or you're simply making green Jell-O for Saint Patrick's Day, the anticipation of a special day can lift your spirits and impart a sense of family tradition to your children.

While toddlers are too young to understand much of the significance of each holiday, you can still make the most of each occasion. Begin by talking to your child about the upcoming event. Read simple library books that explain the story of your tradition. Look at videotapes or photo albums of past family celebrations. When the holiday actually arrives, refer to the books you have read or photos you have looked at to help your child make the connection between the story and the event.

Keep in mind that for toddlers, celebrations do not need to be lavish. Bake a special batch of cookies, paint pictures in seasonal colors, or invite friends over for a simple lunch or teddy-bear tea. To get the most out of the holiday, try to be as routine as possible about your child's meals and naps.

This chapter will suggest many ideas for celebrating holidays with toddlers. Many of the activities break my own rule about simplicity—they're a little complex for most toddlers to do on their own. You'll need to assist and, at times, do part of the process yourself. This does limit the learning value for your child, so try to make these activities the exception rather than the rule. But sometimes it's okay to make or do something just because you want to, rather than wondering and worrying about what your child will learn from it. Toddlers will benefit when you let them do the things they're capable of doing, even if it means not doing everything by themselves.

Birthday Celebrations

Although parents usually emphasize birthdays, most toddlers do not get into birthdays in a really big way. For the first few years of life, a family dinner complete with birthday cake and candles is often sufficient for a birthday celebration. However, if you want to invite a few friends over for a party, keep the festivities simple:

- Put some playdough or a simple craft out to occupy the children until all guests have arrived.
- If there are no other adults on hand, ask the children's parents (or at least one or two) to stay for the party. They'll be a big help to you when it's time to organize the children for food, games, or circle time.
- Serve a simple meal of sandwiches or hot dogs, vegetable sticks, and juice or chocolate milk. If you plan the party for midmorning or afternoon, put out a fruit platter and juice or milk with the birthday cake.
- Most toddlers are too young to enjoy group games, but sitting in a circle singing songs or doing simple finger plays can be great fun.
- After an hour and a half or two hours of eating, singing, playing, and opening gifts, most little guests will be ready to depart. Have your child say good-bye to the guests individually as they leave.

Although sending thank-you notes may be an old-fashioned custom, it's one I started with my children long before they could understand the concept, and it's one I hope they will continue into adulthood. (Good manners and gratitude are never out of date.) Use a piece of your child's artwork as an original thank-you card. Write the message yourself and, if you like, enclose a photograph of your child with each card.

Birthday Memory Book

Construction paper
Stapler
Stickers, glitter, and photograph(s) for decorating
Clear contact paper (optional)
Birthday cards and memorabilia
Glue

Staple or sew together ten (or more) sheets of construction paper to make a birthday memory book for your child. Decorate the front with your child's name, age, birthday date, and so on. Add stickers, glitter, and a photograph of the birthday child, and cover with clear contact paper if you like. Inside the book, your child can glue his birthday cards and other reminders of his special day.

Party Tablecloth

You can use this idea to make custom tablecloths for birthdays, holidays, and other special events. An older child may enjoy making a tablecloth with his friends at his next birthday party.

Large roll or sheets of plain newsprint
Paint, crayons, or markers
Clear vinyl tablecloth

Cut a length of paper the size of the table to be covered. Let your children draw on the paper with crayons, markers, or paints. You may want to add stickers, or you can glue pictures cut from magazines. When the masterpiece is complete, place it on the table and cover with a clear vinyl tablecloth.

Video Time Capsule

If you like this idea, you'll want to begin as early as possible—
your child's first birthday would be the perfect time.

Video camera
Videotape

If you have access to a video camera, consider making a videotape of your child on each birthday throughout his childhood.
Beginning with his first birthday (if you can), spend a couple
of minutes taping him sitting, crawling, standing, walking, or
doing whatever stage he happens to be in. If you like, show his
room, his favorite toys and books, and so on. As the years
progress and your child becomes more vocal, ask him questions about his favorite foods, songs, activities, friends, and so
on. Ask your child what he is looking forward to over the year,
and what he expects life to be like next year on his birthday.
When the segment is complete, put the tape away and don't
tape on it until next year's birthday. If doing this for more than
one child, use a different tape for each, but use the tape only
for the time capsule. Years down the road you'll be able to
watch your child grow up on his video time capsule.

Valentine's Day (February 14)

Valentine's Day is for celebrating love. Although no one is quite sure how Valentine's Day and its accompanying traditions started, most of us enjoy sharing cards, chocolates, hugs, and kisses with those we love on this day.

Valentine celebrations for toddlers can be kept simple. Read a book about Valentine's Day several times in the days and weeks prior to February 14. Make simple red, white, and pink decorations to put up around the house. Bake and ice some heart-shaped cookies to give to a friend or neighbor. On Valentine's Day, dress the whole family in red and put your heart-shaped cookie cutter to work for toast, sandwiches, apples, cheese, and finger Jell-O. A small party with a few friends can be a simple and fun way to celebrate this special day.

Jell-O Painting

1 package red Jell-O
Water
Construction paper
Paintbrush
Scissors

Mix Jell-O with a small amount of water to make a fairly thick, spreadable paste. Cut a heart shape from a piece of construction paper and have your child paint the heart with the Jell-O. Let dry. This makes a delicious-smelling valentine card or picture for someone special.

Valentine Postcard

Heavy white paper or postcard
Paper doily
Red or pink paint
Paintbrush or sponge
Clear contact paper (optional)

Place a paper doily on one side of a blank postcard, or on a piece of heavy white paper folded to make a card. You can hold the doily in place with a small amount of tacky adhesive or a paper clip. Paint or sponge over the doily and onto the postcard beneath it. Remove the doily and let the postcard dry. Cover with clear contact paper to give it a finished look.

Valentine Cookies

Rolled cookie dough
Heart-shaped cookie cutters
Pink icing
Sprinkles or other candy for decorating

Prepare a batch of rolled cookie dough ahead of time. Let your toddler help with some of the simpler parts of the recipe. Roll the dough out and use a heart-shaped cookie cutter to cut heart shapes from the dough. Bake as directed and let cool. Ice with pink icing and decorate with sprinkles or other candy.

Edible Valentines

Graham crackers
Candy conversation hearts, cinnamon hearts, or other heart-
  shaped candy
Frosting

Use frosting to glue candy hearts to graham crackers for a completely edible valentine.

Valentine Cupcakes

Use this idea to make heart-shaped cupcakes for Valentine's Day.

Marbles (1 for each cupcake)
Paper baking cups
Cake batter
Frosting
Sprinkles and other candy for decorating

Wash and dry enough marbles so there's one for each cupcake you're making. Line a muffin tin with paper baking cups. Place one marble in each section between the side of the paper cup and the tin (the marbles mold the baking cups into heart shapes). Pour in the batter and bake according to the recipe. Cool and decorate with frosting, sprinkles, and other candies.

Sweetheart Sandwiches

Bread slices
Softened cream cheese
Red food coloring
Heart-shaped cookie cutters
Honey and/or cinnamon (optional)

Mix softened cream cheese with a drop or two of red food coloring. Add more food coloring, one drop at a time, if you want a darker color. If you like, flavor the cream cheese with honey and/or cinnamon. Spread the colored cream cheese on slices of bread. Use cookie cutters to cut out heart-shaped sandwiches.

Valentine Heart

Pink construction paper
Scissors
Red and white liquid tempera paint
Spoons
Small rolling pin (optional)

Cut out large heart shapes from construction paper; fold in half, then open again. Have your child use a spoon to dribble red and white liquid tempera paint onto the heart. Fold the heart up with the paint on the inside; your child can use his hand or a small rolling pin to press on the top of the folded heart. Open up the heart again to see the designs the paint has made. You can write on the unpainted side of the heart, or glue it onto another sheet of white or red construction paper to make a pretty Valentine's Day card.

Saint Patrick's Day (March 17)

Saint Patrick's Day is set aside to honor the patron saint of Ireland. Bishop Patrick introduced Christianity to Ireland during the fifth century, and in Ireland he is still honored with a national holiday and a week of religious festivities.

Whether you're Irish or not, Saint Patrick's Day can help break up the monotony of the last days of winter. Dress in green and invite a few friends over for a small Saint Patrick's Day celebration. Make a craft together and play a few simple games. Serve green food such as cupcakes or sugar cookies with green icing (or decorate them as a party activity). Color white grape juice green with a drop or two of food coloring, or serve limeade or green Kool-Aid. Wind up the day with your own Saint Patrick's Day parade either in your living room or outside if the weather is fine.

Potato Press Picture

Raw potato, cut in half
Shallow dish of green tempera paint
Construction paper

Dip the cut surface of the potato into the green paint and press onto the construction paper. Remind your child to press the potato onto the paper gently. Repeat until the paper is covered with green shapes. Use as a Saint Patrick's Day card or picture.

Shamrock Rubbings

Sandpaper
Scissors
Crayons
Paper

Cut shamrock shapes out of sandpaper. Use different grains of sandpaper and cut the shamrocks in several different sizes. Tape the shamrocks to a table. Show your child how to place his paper over the shamrock and rub with the side of a crayon to get a Saint Patrick's Day design.

Shamrock Necklace

Green and white construction paper
Scissors
Hole punch
Shoelaces, ribbon, or yarn for stringing

Cut several sizes of shamrocks from green and white construction paper. Punch a hole in the top of each shamrock.
Give your child a shoelace (or length of ribbon, or yarn with
masking tape wrapped on each end) and show him how to
string the shamrocks to make a Saint Patrick's Day necklace.

Easter (Date Varies)

Easter is a joyous celebration, the traditional Christian holiday that celebrates the resurrection of Jesus Christ. It is also a time to celebrate the coming of spring and all the delightful signs of new life that abound. Easter is a great time for family dinners and small get-togethers with friends. Decorate Easter eggs together or make a simple Easter craft. Hold an Easter egg or candy hunt outoors or in, depending on the weather. Have an informal parade in your neighborhood with decorated wagons and tricycles. This is another wonderful holiday that helps break the monotony of the last few days of winter, so start your Easter crafts and activities early.

Easy Easter Eggs

These Easter eggs are easy enough for even the littlest hands to make.

Cotton swabs
Cotton balls
Liquid tempera paint
Hard-boiled eggs
Clear acrylic spray (optional)

Dip a cotton swab or cotton ball in paint and use to dab paint on the hard-boiled egg. For a shiny finish, spray with clear acrylic spray.

Tissue Easter Egg

Colored tissue paper cut into 3-inch squares
Construction paper
Scissors
Glue

Cut an egg shape from a piece of construction paper. Show your child how to wad the tissue paper square, dip it in glue, and stick it to the egg.

Easter Bouquet

Paper baking cups
Scissors
Pipe cleaners
Glue
Ribbon
Glitter

Poke a hole with scissors or a pen through the bottom of the baking cup. Stick a pipe cleaner through the hole. Bend the top of the pipe cleaner over and glue into place. Spread glue over the paper baking cup and decorate with glitter. Bunch together four or five flowers, twisting the pipe cleaner stems together. Tie with ribbon to make a springtime bouquet.

Tissue Paper Eggs

Colored tissue paper
White craft glue
Hard-boiled eggs
Clear acrylic spray (optional)

Tear colored tissue paper into small pieces. Dilute white craft glue with a few drops of water. Have your child spread glue on the hard-boiled egg with his fingers. After he has washed his hands, show him how to gently press pieces of tissue paper onto the egg. Cover with a light coating of glue or spray with clear acrylic spray.

Easter Egg Pickup

Tissue paper
Pie plate
Plastic drinking straws
Scissors

Cut several tissue paper eggs about three inches long. Place the eggs in a pie plate. Show your child how to put the straw to his mouth and take a deep breath, seeing how many eggs he can pick up on the end of the straw.

Easter Egg Holder

This is an easy way to display all the eggs your child decorates.

Empty paper towel roll
Scissors
Construction paper
Glue
Glitter or stickers for decorating

Cut the paper towel roll into 2-inch sections. Cut strips of construction paper 2 inches wide and long enough to wrap around the paper towel roll. Glue the construction paper strips to the pieces of paper towel roll, and decorate with glitter or stickers.

Easter Egg Necklace

Construction paper in several different colors
Scissors
Hole punch
Shoelace, ribbon, or yarn
Glue, glitter, sequins, or stickers (optional)

Cut out some egg-shaped pieces of construction paper in several different colors. Punch a hole in the top of each egg. If you like, decorate with crayons, markers, stickers, glitter, or sequins. Show your child how to slip the end of the shoelace through the holes in the eggs to make a necklace. You'll need to tie something temporarily onto one end of the shoelace to make sure the eggs don't fall off the other end as he adds them. If using ribbon or yarn, taping the end makes it easier for little fingers to thread it through the hole.

Independence Day (July 4)

Independence Day celebrates the anniversary of the signing of the Declaration of Independence in 1776, and so this holiday is the birthday of the United States. Independence Day celebrations differ from family to family, although traditions usually include a parade, picnic, or barbecue with family and friends and fireworks at night.

Most toddlers won't understand the significance of their own birthday, so celebrating the birthday of a country is not a concept they will easily grasp. You can, however, do simple things to begin building Independence Day traditions with your child. Make a birthday card for the United States using some of your child's artwork. Bake a birthday cake, light a few candles, and sing "Happy Birthday" to the United States. Fly the flag proudly. You can decorate your house and dress your children with a red, white, and blue theme. Your family's Independence Day traditions and celebrations will help your children feel proud of their country.

Stars and Stripes Sponge Painting

Star- and stripe-shaped sponges
Red and blue liquid tempera paint
White construction paper

Dip the star- and stripe-shaped sponges into red and blue liquid tempera paint. Press onto a piece of white construction paper for a stars and stripes painting.

Fireworks Printing

3 plastic scouring pads (1 for each color)
Red, white, and blue liquid tempera paint
Black construction paper

Pour the paint into three flat containers. Dip a plastic scouring pad into one of the paint containers and press it onto a piece of black construction paper. (Encourage your child to press gently rather than pound his scouring pad onto the paper.) Continue dipping and pressing, using all three colors to create an Independence Day fireworks picture.

Fourth of July Salad

Raspberries
Blueberries
Vanilla yogurt

Combine raspberries, blueberries, and vanilla yogurt in a small bowl. Mix and serve.

Flag Snacks

Graham crackers
White frosting
3 small containers
Red and blue food coloring
Small plastic knives or Popsicle sticks

Divide white frosting equally into three small containers. Add
a few drops of red food coloring to one container and a few
drops of blue food coloring to another. Mix well. If you like,
add more food coloring until the desired shades are reached.
Show your toddlers how to use a small plastic knife or Popsicle
stick to spread the colored frosting onto graham crackers.

Halloween (October 31)

Halloween began in ancient times as a pagan celebration of the arrival of winter. It was then that the Lord of Death called together all the souls of the wicked who had died during the past year. The Druids believed that on this night ghosts, goblins, and witches would appear and harm people. Huge bonfires and masks were meant to frighten away these evil beings. People dressed in costumes of animal skins so that the spirits wouldn't recognize them. Special food left on the doorstep to appease the spirits began our tradition of trick-or-treating.

Despite its frightening origins, Halloween has become a fun tradition for many people—adults and children alike. As with most other holidays, toddlers are too young to understand the significance of Halloween. They can, however, be easily frightened by some of the activities which surround this day, so it's wise to be careful where you take them at this time of year. Churches and community centers often have fall carnivals or parties where children can play games, eat food, and have fun without the dangers associated with trick-or-treating. If you want to have a small Halloween party yourself, encourage friends to dress in fun, nonscary costumes. Make a simple craft, then decorate and eat some Halloween cookies, cupcakes, or other treats.

Regardless of how you celebrate this occasion, here are some fun activities for you and your child to do together.

Jack-o'-Orange

Orange
Whole cloves
Black marker

Use a black marker to draw a simple face on an orange. Show your child how to poke the cloves into the orange to make a Halloween face.

Painted Spider Web

White tempera paint
Black construction paper
Drinking straw

Drop a bit of thin white tempera paint onto the center of a piece of black construction paper. Give your child a straw and show him how to blow the paint around to make a spider web.

Paper Bag Pumpkin

Paper lunch bag
Newspaper or other paper for crumpling
Twist tie, rubber band, or string
Orange and green tempera paint
Paintbrush
Black marker

Crumple up newspaper or other scraps of paper and stuff the lunch bag until it is about two-thirds full. Close the bag with a twist tie, rubber band, or piece of string. Twist the unstuffed part of the bag to make a stem. Paint the pumpkin part of the bag orange, and paint the stem green. When the paint is dry, draw a face on the pumpkin with a black marker.

Paper Plate Spider Web

Even if you're not into spiders at Halloween, this is a neat idea for any time of the year.

Paper plate
Pie plate or round cake pan
Black paint
Marble

Place a paper plate inside a metal or aluminum pie plate or round cake pan. Put a small amount of black paint in the center of the paper plate and drop a marble in. Your child will have fun moving and tilting the pie plate or cake pan from side to side to make a spider web on his plate.

For a variation, paint the paper plate dark blue or black first and use white paint for a more realistic looking spider web, or use more than one color of paint for a rainbow spider web.

Pumpkin Prints

Very small pumpkin
Knife
Orange and black tempera paint
Paper

Cut a small pumpkin in half and dip it into orange and black paint. Press it onto paper to make a pumpkin print. When the paint dries, cover with clear contact paper for a Halloween place mat, or fold the paper in half to make a Halloween card.

Thanksgiving (Fourth Thursday in November)

The first Thanksgiving celebration was held by the Pilgrims after their first harvest in 1621. Although many of the original settlers died that first year, the remaining Pilgrims were grateful for the abundance of their harvest and invited their Native American neighbors to join in their three-day feast.

Thanksgiving celebrations today usually include a huge family meal of roast turkey and all the trimmings. Although your toddler will not understand the significance of this holiday, it is never too early to begin to cultivate a spirit of thankfulness in your child. He may not understand all that you say, but you can still talk with your child about all that you have for which you are thankful.

You can also begin to encourage a giving spirit in your child. Donate canned food to your local food bank. It's a simple act that will positively impact your community. Prepare for Thanksgiving each year by setting aside good, usable cothing and toys and taking them to a local relief agency. Bake a plate of cookies for housebound friends or community workers. Several years ago we surprised the garbage collectors one morning with a plate of brownies. My kids still talk about it!

Feather Printing

Sponges
Scissors
Liquid tempera paint (in fall colors)
Water
Paper

Cut feather shapes in various sizes out of sponges, being sure to include the stem on the end of the feather shape you cut. Wet sponges, squeeze out, dip into paint, and press onto large sheets of paper. The different sizes and colors of feathers create a nice effect.

Thanksgiving Place Mat

Old magazines
Construction paper or light cardboard
Glue or paste
Clear contact paper

Give your child old magazines and have him cut out things for which he is thankful. Let him glue them onto a piece of cardboard or construction paper and cover with clear contact paper for a Thanksgiving place mat.

Thanksgiving Turkey

Construction paper or small paper plate
Marker or pencil
Glue
Dried beans and uncooked pasta

Trace around your child's hand (fingers spread out) on a piece
of construction paper or small paper plate. Using the pen or
marker, draw an eye and beak on the thumb and turkey feet at
the bottom of the traced hand. Decorate by gluing on dried
beans and uncooked pasta.

Dry Leaf Collage

Construction paper
Scissors
Dry leaves
Glue stick

Cut one or two leaf shapes out of construction paper. Crinkle up dry leaves until they're in fairly small pieces (this may be your toddler's favorite part). Spread glue on one side of the construction paper leaf and sprinkle with dry leaf pieces. If you like, punch a hole in the construction paper and hang to display.

Rainbow Turkey

Brown, red, yellow, and green paint
Paper
Markers

Paint your child's palm and thumb brown, then paint strips of red, yellow, and green across his fingers (like a rainbow). Press his hand on a piece of paper to make a turkey print. When the paint is dry, use markers to add the eye, beak, and feet.

Christmas (December 25)

Christmas is a time when Christians the world over celebrate the birth of Jesus Christ. For some, Christmas means the arrival of Santa Claus, Father Christmas, Père Noël, or Saint Nicholas. Christmas celebrations usually emphasize family togetherness, doing thoughtful and loving things for others, and lots of good food.

However Christmas is celebrated, most will agree that this time of year often brings with it more than peace, joy, love, and goodwill. For adults, Christmas often means a time of frenzied activity, extra stress, and financial demands that can be hard to meet. Sometimes unrealistic expectations—those we have of ourselves, those we have of others, and those others have of us—make it hard to truly enjoy the wonders of the season.

At this busy time of year, concentrate on what is important. Spend your time, money, and energy on activities that will build or uphold family traditions and make memories for your child. Don't forget simple pleasures like reading together, singing carols by the Christmas tree, or making a holiday craft. Bake some Christmas cookies together, go for a walk in the snow, and sip hot chocolate by the fire. Children need your time and attention more than anything else. Although your child may soon forget toys and other material things, time spent together makes memories he will treasure for a lifetime.

As with other holiday crafts in this chapter, some of these activities may be too complex for some toddlers. Remember to allow your child to do the parts he is capable of doing. Simple painting projects or tissue paper collages in seasonal colors are also great Christmas activities for toddlers.

Christmas Noisemaker

Empty frozen-juice container with metal lid
Glue gun or tape
Popped popcorn
Uncooked white beans

Put uncooked beans and popped popcorn into a clean, dry frozen-juice container. Place the metal lid on top and glue or tape securely. If you like, cover the juice container with red or green construction paper and decorate with markers or stickers. Now your child has a Christmas noisemaker to shake, shake, shake.

Cotton Ball Snowman

Cotton balls
Clear contact paper
Construction paper
Scissors
Stapler

Cut three circles from clear contact paper. The circles should be in three different sizes ranging from a diameter of 1½–2 inches to 4½–5 inches. Staple the contact paper, backing side up, to the construction paper to form a snowman shape. Your child can peel off the backing and stick cotton balls to the contact paper to cover the snowman. If you like, cut additional snowman features such as a hat or carrot from construction paper and glue to the snowman.

Cinnamon Drawing

Sandpaper
Scissors
Cinnamon sticks

Cut the sandpaper into a holiday shape such as a star, Christmas tree, or gingerbread man. Show your child how to rub the cinnamon stick on the sandpaper to make both a nice design and a pleasing fragrance. If you like, punch a hole at the top of the sandpaper and string yarn through it to make a Christmas tree decoration.

Animal Dress-Up

Stuffed animals or dolls
Christmas ribbon, bows, or fabric

When decorating your home for the holidays, encourage your child to do some decorating of his own. Dress up your child's favorite dolls or stuffed animals with some Christmas ribbon or big bright bows or use Christmas fabric to create scarves or kerchiefs. Display the animals on a shelf in your child's room or on a mantel in a more prominent part of your house.

Pencil Holder

Tape and toddlers are a great combination. Your child will have fun making this pencil holder (or vase) as a Christmas gift for a family member or friend.

Small, clean can
Masking tape
Brown liquid shoe polish or tempera paint
Clear acrylic spray or shellac

Show your toddler how to tear small pieces of masking tape and stick them onto a small can. If your toddler has trouble tearing the tape, tear the tape for him and place the pieces around the rim of an upside-down tuna can or plastic container. When the can is covered with pieces of masking tape, paint with brown liquid shoe polish or tempera paint to create a leathery look. If brown isn't high on your child's list of favorite colors, choose another color. When the paint or shoe polish is dry, spray with clear acrylic spray, or brush with shellac to give the pencil holder a shiny finish.

Christmas Tree

Lids from frozen-juice cans or baby-food jars (at least 10)
Magnet strips
Glue gun
Green felt
Felt in other bright colors
Scissors

Cut small circles of colored felt to fit the lids. Use lots of green and other colors such as red, yellow, and blue. If using baby-food jar lids, glue a circle of felt to the inside of each lid. If using juice container lids, glue the felt to the outside of the lid. Glue a small magnetic strip to the other side of each lid. You can arrange these magnets in the shape of a Christmas tree on your refrigerator door. Your toddler will have fun making designs of his own.

Christmas Doorknob Decoration

Red felt
Plastic lid for tracing, about 4 inches in diameter
Green felt
Glue
Stickers, glitter, beads, sequins, and so on

Cut a 4-inch circle out of red felt. Cut out a 1-inch circle in the middle of the red circle, and cut four ½-inch slits outward from the inner circle to allow it to fit over a doorknob. Cut a 7-inch Christmas tree shape from the green felt. Glue the top of the tree to the bottom of the red felt circle. Your child can decorate his tree with beads, glitter, sequins, stickers, or any other scraps you have on hand.

Rudolph Sandwiches

Sliced bread
Peanut butter
Pretzels
Raisins
Maraschino cherry

Cut a slice of bread into a triangle shape. Spread the triangle of bread with peanut butter (or use jam, honey, or cream cheese according to your child's preference). Add pretzels for antlers, raisins for eyes, and a bright red maraschino cherry for Rudolph's nose.

Christmas Bag

Your child can use this bag to wrap a gift in, or you can have one on hand for each member of the family on Christmas morning. It will help keep cards and small, opened gifts from getting lost in the sea of boxes, gift-wrap, and presents.

Large paper bag
Glue
Bits of wrapping paper, stickers, ribbon, fabric, and
  Christmas cards

Spread glue on one side of a large paper bag. Let your child stick whatever materials you have handy on the bag: small pieces of holiday wrapping paper, seasonal stickers, ribbon, fabric, or pictures cut from old Christmas cards. If you like, decorate the other side of the bag in the same way.

Smelly Christmas Tree

Construction paper
Scissors
Glue
One package green Jell-O
Empty salt shaker or spice container
Paintbrush
Hole punch (optional)
Ribbon or string (optional)

Cut a Christmas tree shape from a piece of construction paper.
Use the paintbrush to spread glue all over the tree. Sprinkle
Jell-O powder onto the glue. Shake off excess Jell-O and let
dry. Use as a Christmas card or punch a hole in the top of the
tree, insert a loop of ribbon or string through the hole, and
use as a Christmas tree ornament.

Gingerbread People

1 cup shortening
¾ cup honey
1 egg
1 cup molasses
1½ teaspoon baking soda
½ teaspoon salt
2 teaspoons ground ginger
1 teaspoon cinnamon
1 teaspoon ground cloves
5 cups flour
Raisins, nuts, licorice, and small candies for decorating

Mix shortening, honey, egg, and molasses. Sift soda, salt, ginger, cinnamon, cloves, and flour together. Mix wet and dry ingredients. Refrigerate dough until cold. Roll out chilled dough ¼ inch thick on a floured surface. Cut with a gingerbread-person cookie cutter. Decorate with raisins, nuts, licorice, and other small candies. Bake at 375°F for 10 minutes.

If you like, bake the gingerbread people ahead of time, and let your child decorate the cooled cookies with icing and small candies. If your family isn't fond of gingerbread, don't let that stop you. Substitute another rolled cookie dough recipe instead.

Stone Paperweight

This paperweight is easy for toddlers to make and a great Christmas gift for someone special.

Large, smooth stone
Tempera paint
Paintbrush
Shellac
Glitter (optional)

Go on a walk with your toddler and look for a large, smooth stone. At home, have your child paint the stone in his favorite colors. When dry, brush with shellac for a shiny finish. If you like, sprinkle glitter on the shellac before it dries.

Krispie Christmas Treats

5 cups Rice Krispies
¼ cup butter or margarine
4 cups mini-marshmallows (or 40 large marshmallows)
Red or green food coloring
Metal cookie cutters in Christmas shapes

Melt margarine in a 3-quart saucepan, then add marshmallows and cook over low heat, stirring constantly until syrupy. Add food coloring and stir until the color is well mixed in. Remove from heat, add cereal, and stir until well coated. Press into a cookie sheet and let cool. Use metal Christmas-shaped cookie cutters to cut out some Christmas treats.

Hanukkah (Date Varies)

Hanukkah, the most joyous and festive of Jewish holidays, lasts eight days and takes place in December—sometimes early and sometimes late in the month.

Hanukkah, which means "dedication," was first celebrated more than two thousand years ago. Hanukkah commemorates a time when the Holy Temple in Jerusalem had been restored and was about to be rededicated. Only one day's supply of oil for the holy lamps was found, but the lamps miraculously burned for eight days! This is why Hanukkah is also called the Festival of Lights, and why the main focus of the celebration is the lighting of candles. A menorah, a special nine-branch candelabrum, is used each day throughout the celebration.

Every year Jews all over the world celebrate Hanukkah. Families gather to light the Hanukkah menorah, remember their ancestors' historic struggle for religious freedom, and recite prayers of thanks to God. Family members exchange gifts, eat special foods, play games, and retell the story of Hanukkah.

Hanukkah Rubbings

Posterboard or Hanukkah cards with
* raised Hanukkah symbols*
Scissors
Paper
Crayons

Cut Hanukkah symbols from posterboard or use Hanukkah cards with raised Hanukkah symbols on the front. Place the cutouts on the table, put paper over them, and show your child how to rub a crayon sideways over the paper to create a rubbing of the symbol beneath. Some significant Hanukkah symbols include candles, a menorah, a Star of David (six-pointed star), an elephant, and a hammer.

Star of David

2 yellow pipe cleaners or 6 Popsicle sticks
Glue
Glitter
Yarn or ribbon

Bend each of two pipe cleaners into a triangle, twisting the ends together securely. If using Popsicle sticks, glue into two triangle shapes. Place one triangle upside down on the other. Spread glue at the points where the triangles meet. Let dry. If using Popsicle sticks, paint them yellow if you like. Dab glue onto the star and sprinkle on glitter. Use yarn or ribbon to hang the star from the top of a window or in a doorway.

Handprint Menorah

Most one-year-olds will not sit still long enough for this activity, but most two- and three-year-olds will enjoy it.

White, yellow, and orange tempera paint
Blue construction paper

Paint the palms of your child's hands white (the candleholder), his fingers yellow (the candles), and the tips of his fingers orange (the flames). Cross his hands over and press them onto the blue construction paper (his thumbs will be on opposite ends of the paper). Make sure his pinky fingers overlap and print as one finger, so the total number of imprints is nine. You could fold the construction paper in half before printing and use it for a Hanukkah card, or cover it with clear contact paper for a Hanukkah place mat.

Egg Carton Menorah

Empty egg carton
Scissors
Glue, tape, or stapler
Blue and yellow tempera paint
Q-Tips

Divide an egg carton in half lengthwise to make two strips of six sections each. Cut three sections from one strip and glue, tape, or staple to the other strip so that you have one strip with nine sections. Paint the nine-section strip blue. Make candles by dipping nine Q-Tips into yellow paint. Poke one through the top of each section.

Older children may enjoy using birthday candles in place of Q-Tips. If you decide to actually light the birthday candles, be sure to supervise carefully. If you find the candles a little loose, secure them by wrapping playdough around the base of the candle where it pokes through the egg carton.

Kwanzaa (December 26 to January 1)

Kwanzaa, a seven-day African-American celebration, takes place each year from December 26 to January 1. Kwanzaa, which means "first fruit," is based on the traditional African winter harvest festival and is not a religious holiday. During this time, African Americans reflect upon the year that is ending and take pride in their African heritage.

Kwanzaa begins the day after Christmas, but the two celebrations are very different. Kwanzaa celebrates the harvest and a way of life handed down by ancestors and parents. Although special handmade gifts or educational games and books are exchanged, values—rather than gifts—are emphasized. Seven principles or values are celebrated, one for each day of the Kwanzaa week. These are unity, self-determination, collective work and responsibility, cooperative economics, purpose, creativity, and faith.

Whether or not your family celebrates Kwanzaa, you may enjoy trying a few simple Kwanzaa activities with your child. The following ideas are fun and easy to do.

Pasta Necklace

Ziti noodles
Red, green, and black tempera paint
Paintbrushes
Clear acrylic spray (optional)
Shoelaces, ribbon, yarn, or thin elastic cord

Paint ziti noodles with red, green, and black tempera paint.
Allow to dry. Spray with clear acrylic spray if you like.
(Alternatively, you could use spray paint or dye the noodles
using the Pasta Dye recipe on page 363.) Give your child a
shoelace (or a piece of ribbon, yarn, or thin elastic cord) with
a piece of masking tape wrapped around one end. Show him
how to thread it through the noodles to make a colorful
Kwanzaa necklace.

Kwanzaa Shapes

Black construction paper
Scissors
Red and green tissue paper or gift-wrap
Glue
Glitter (optional)
Hole punch (optional)
Ribbon or yarn (optional)

Cut circles, squares, rectangles, and triangles out of black construction paper. Cut or tear red and green tissue paper or gift-wrap into fairly small (about 1-inch) pieces. Spread glue on the black construction paper shapes, and press the tissue paper or gift-wrap pieces onto the glue. If you like, sprinkle glitter on for a sparkly effect. Punch a hole in the top of each shape, thread a loop of ribbon or yarn through the hole, and hang from doorknobs, or use the shapes to make Kwanzaa cards.

Kwanzaa Chain

Red, green, and black construction paper
Scissors
Glue or paste

Cut strips of red, green, and black construction paper 3–4 inches long and ½–1 inch wide. Have your child form a circle with one strip, gluing the ends together. Take the next strip and loop it through the first circle, again gluing the ends together. Tell him to continue looping and gluing until the chain is the length he wants. Use to decorate doorways, walls, and so on.

Corncob Painting

Corn is a traditional part of the Kwanzaa celebration. Fresh corn is difficult (or impossible) to get at this time of year, so use a dried corncob for this activity.

Paper
Flat box (the kind a 24-pack of soda comes in)
  or large baking pan
Red, green, and black liquid tempera paint
Flat container for paint (big enough to fit the corn)
Corncob (husk removed)
Clear contact paper (optional)

Place a sheet of paper in the flat box or baking pan. Pour the liquid tempera paint into a shallow, flat container. Place one whole corncob into the paint. Roll the corncob around so that it is completely covered with paint. Place the paint-covered corncob in the box with the paper and let your child rotate the box around so that the corncob rolls from side to side. If you like, use another corncob in a different color paint and repeat the rolling process until your child decides he is done.

Let the painting dry. If you like, cover with clear contact paper and use as a Kwanzaa place mat. For variety, use only red and green paint on a piece of black construction paper.

Appendix A

Basic Craft Recipes

Although your toddler is still quite young, she is already beginning to develop creative skills. She undoubtedly loves to scribble on paper (or walls) and already may have experienced the joy of fingerpainting. You have probably noticed that she doesn't care as much for *what* she makes as for the process of working with materials of different colors and textures. Whether it's the process or the product that interests your child, the craft materials in this appendix are essential for her artwork. On the following pages you'll find easy recipes for paint, glue, paste, modeling compounds, and more.

PAINT

Each of these nine recipes will produce a good-quality paint for your child's use. The ingredients and preparation vary from recipe to recipe, so choose one that best suits the supplies and time you have available.

When mixing paint, keep in mind the age of your young artist. As a general rule, younger children require thicker paint and brushes. Paint should always be stored in covered containers. Small plastic spillproof paint containers are available at art supply stores. Each comes with an airtight lid, holds brushes upright without tipping, and is well worth the purchase price of several dollars.

Flour-Based Poster Paint

¼ cup flour
1 cup water
Small jars or plastic containers
3 tablespoons powdered tempera paint per container
2 tablespoons water per container
½ teaspoon liquid starch or liquid detergent per container
  (optional)

Measure flour into saucepan. Slowly add 1 cup water while stirring to make a smooth paste. Heat, stirring constantly, until paste begins to thicken. Cool. Measure ¼ cup paste into each small container. Add 3 tablespoons powdered tempera paint and 2 tablespoons water to each container. For a matte finish, add liquid starch. For a glossy finish, add liquid detergent. Store covered.

Cornstarch Paint

Medium saucepan
½ cup cornstarch
½ cup cold water
4 cups boiling water
Small jars or plastic containers
Tempera paint, dry or liquid

Measure cornstarch into saucepan. Add cold water to cornstarch and stir to make a smooth paste. Stir in boiling water.

Place saucepan over medium-low heat and stir until boiling. Boil 1 minute; remove from heat. Cool. Spoon about ½ cup of thickened cornstarch mixture into each container, using a different cup for each color. For each color, stir 1 teaspoon dry tempera or 1 tablespoon liquid tempera into cornstarch mixture. (Use more paint for more intense color.) If paint is too thick, stir in 1 teaspoon water at a time until desired consistency is achieved. Store in refrigerator. This recipe makes about 4 cups of paint.

Detergent Poster Paint
Small jars or plastic containers
1 tablespoon clear liquid detergent per container
2 teaspoons powdered tempera paint per container

In each small container, mix together 1 tablespoon liquid detergent and 2 teaspoons powdered tempera paint. This recipe makes enough for one painting session.

Condensed-Milk Paint
Bowl
1 cup condensed milk
Food coloring

In bowl, mix 1 cup condensed milk with many drops of food coloring to make a very bright, glossy paint. This paint is not intended to be eaten, but it won't harm a child who decides to make a snack of it. Store covered in refrigerator.

Homemade Face Paint

Small jars or plastic containers
1 teaspoon cornstarch per container
½ teaspoon cold cream per container
½ teaspoon water per container
Food coloring

In each small container, mix cornstarch and cold cream until well blended. Add water and stir. Add food coloring one drop at a time until you get the desired color. Paint small designs on face with a small paintbrush; remove with soap and water. Store covered.

Halloween Face Paint

Bowl
1 tablespoon solid shortening
2 tablespoons cornstarch
Food coloring
Water (optional)
Small jar or plastic container

In bowl, mix shortening and cornstarch until smooth. Add food coloring one drop at a time until you get the desired color. Use a sponge or fingers to apply paint to a large area, such as an entire face. To apply with a small brush, thin paint with a little water first. Remove with soap and water. Store covered.

Edible Egg-Yolk Paint
Small jars or plastic containers
1 egg yolk per container
¼ teaspoon water per container
Food coloring

In each small container, mix one egg yolk with ¼ teaspoon water and many drops of food coloring. Use a paintbrush to apply paint to freshly baked cookies; return cookies to oven until paint hardens.

Cornstarch Fingerpaint
3 tablespoons sugar
½ cup cornstarch
Medium saucepan
2 cups cold water
Muffin tin or small cups
Food coloring
Soap flakes or liquid dishwashing detergent

Mix sugar and cornstarch in saucepan. Turn heat on low, add cold water, and stir until mixture is thick. Remove from heat. Divide mixture into four or five portions, spooning into muffin-tin sections or small cups. Add a few drops of food coloring and a pinch of soap flakes or a drop of liquid dishwashing detergent to each portion. Stir and let cool before use. Store covered.

Flour Fingerpaint
1 cup flour
2 tablespoons salt
Saucepan
1½ cups cold water
Wire whisk or eggbeater
1¼ cups hot water
Food coloring or tempera paint

Put flour and salt in saucepan. Add cold water and beat with whisk or eggbeater until smooth. Add hot water and boil until mixture is thick. Beat again until smooth. Color as desired with food coloring or powdered tempera paint. Store covered in refrigerator.

PLAYDOUGH

Everyone seems to have a favorite playdough recipe, and many old favorites have been included here. Some require cooking and some don't; some are meant to be eaten and some are not. Choose the recipe that best suits your needs and the ingredients you have on hand. Store playdough in a covered container or Ziploc bag. If it sweats a little, just add more flour. For sensory variety, use playdough warm or cool as well as at room temperature.

Oatmeal Playdough
1 part flour
1 part water
2 parts oatmeal
Bowl

Combine all ingredients in a bowl; mix well and knead until smooth. This playdough is not intended to be eaten, but it will not hurt a child who decides to taste it. Store covered in refrigerator. Your child can make this playdough without help; however, it doesn't last as long as cooked playdough.

Uncooked Playdough
Bowl
1 cup cold water
1 cup salt
2 teaspoons vegetable oil
Tempera paint or food coloring
3 cups flour
2 tablespoons cornstarch

In bowl, mix water, salt, oil, and enough tempera paint or food coloring to make a bright color. Gradually add flour and cornstarch until the mixture reaches the consistency of bread dough. Store covered.

Peanut Butter Playdough

2 cups peanut butter
6 tablespoons honey
Nonfat dry milk or milk plus flour
Cocoa or carob for chocolate flavor (optional)
Edible treats for decoration

Combine all ingredients in a bowl and mix, adding enough
dry milk or milk plus flour to reach the consistency of bread
dough. Add cocoa or carob, if desired. Shape, decorate with
edible treats, and eat!

Salt Playdough

1 cup salt
1 cup water
½ cup flour plus additional flour
Saucepan

Mix salt, water, and flour in saucepan and cook over medium
heat. Remove from heat when mixture is thick and rubbery.
As the mixture cools, knead in enough flour to make the
dough workable.

Colored Playdough

1 cup water
1 tablespoon vegetable oil
½ cup salt
1 tablespoon cream of tartar
Food coloring
Saucepan
1 cup flour

Combine water, oil, salt, cream of tartar, and food coloring in a saucepan and heat until warm. Remove from heat and add flour. Stir, then knead until smooth. The cream of tartar makes this dough last 6 months or longer, so resist the temptation to omit this ingredient if you don't have it on hand. Store this dough in an airtight container or a Ziploc freezer bag.

Kool-Aid Playdough

½ cup salt
2 cups water
Saucepan
Food coloring, tempera powder, or Kool-Aid powder for color
2 tablespoons vegetable oil
2 cups sifted flour
2 tablespoons alum

Combine salt and water in saucepan and boil until salt dissolves. Remove from heat and tint with food coloring, tempera powder, or Kool-Aid. Add oil, flour, and alum. Knead until smooth. This dough will last 2 months or longer.

CLAY

Use the following recipes to make clay that can be rolled or shaped into sculptures. Some clays should be dried overnight, while others are best baked in an oven. When hard, sculptures can be decorated and preserved with acrylic paint or finish.

Modeling Clay
2 cups salt
⅔ cups water
Saucepan
1 cup cornstarch
½ cup cold water

Stir salt and water in a saucepan over heat 4–5 minutes. Remove from heat; add cornstarch and cold water. Stir until smooth; return to heat and cook until thick. Allow the clay to cool, then shape as desired. When dry, decorate with paint, markers, glitter, and so on. If you like, finish with clear acrylic spray or clear nail polish. Store unused clay in a Ziploc bag.

Bread Clay

6 slices white bread, crusts removed
6 tablespoons white glue
½ teaspoon detergent or 2 teaspoons glycerine
Food coloring
Paintbrush
Equal parts white glue and water
Acrylic paint or spray or clear nail polish

Knead bread with glue plus detergent or glycerine until the mixture is no longer sticky. Separate into portions and tint with food coloring. Let your child shape the clay. Brush the sculpture with equal parts glue and water for a smooth appearance. Let dry overnight. Use acrylic paints or spray or clear nail polish to seal and preserve.

Baker's Clay

4 cups flour
1 cup salt
1 teaspoon alum
1½ cups water
Food coloring (optional)
Large bowl
Cookie cutters, drinking straw, and fine wire (optional)
Baking sheet
Fine sandpaper
Plastic-based poster paint, acrylic paint, or markers
Clear shellac, acrylic spray, or nail polish

Mix flour, salt, alum, and water in bowl. If dough is too dry, knead in another tablespoon of water. Dough can be colored by dividing it into several parts and kneading a few drops of food coloring into each part. Roll or mold into ornaments.

To roll: Roll dough ⅛ inch thick on a lightly floured surface. Cut with cookie cutters dipped in flour. Make a hole for hanging by dipping the end of a drinking straw in flour and using the straw to cut a tiny circle ¼ inch from the ornament's edge. You can also use the straw to cut more clay dots for use as decorations.

To mold: Shape dough into figures such as flowers, fruits, animals, and so on. The figures should be no more than ½ inch thick.

Insert fine wire in ornaments for hanging. Bake ornaments on an ungreased baking sheet for about 30 minutes at 250°F. Turn and bake another 90 minutes until hard and dry. Remove from oven and cool, then smooth with fine sandpaper. Decorate both sides of ornaments with plastic-based poster paint, acrylic paint, or markers. Let dry and seal with clear shellac, acrylic spray, or nail polish.

Makes about five dozen 2½-inch ornaments.

No-Bake Craft Clay
1 cup cornstarch
1¼ cups cold water
2 cups baking soda (1 pound)
Saucepan

Food coloring (optional)
Plate
Damp cloth
Tempera or acrylic paints (optional)
Clear shellac, acrylic spray, or nail polish

Combine cornstarch, water, and baking soda in saucepan; stir over medium heat for about 4 minutes until mixture thickens to a moist mashed-potato consistency. (For colored clay, add a few drops of food coloring to the water before it is mixed with cornstarch and baking soda.) Remove from heat, turn onto plate, and cover with a damp cloth until cool. Knead until smooth. Shape as desired or store in an airtight container or Ziploc bag. Dry sculptures overnight, then paint with tempera or acrylic. Seal with shellac, acrylic spray, or nail polish.

No-Bake Cookie Clay
2 cups salt
⅔ cup water
Medium saucepan
1 cup cornstarch
½ cup cold water
Rolling pin
Cookie cutters
Drinking straw
Paint, glitter, and other decorative materials

Mix salt with ⅔ cup water in saucepan. Stir and boil until salt dissolves. Remove from heat. Add cornstarch and ½ cup cold water and stir. If mixture doesn't immediately thicken, heat and stir until it does. Sprinkle cornstarch on table and rolling pin. Roll out clay and cut with cookie cutters. Use straw to make holes for hanging. Let dry overnight and decorate with paint, glitter, and so on. Remind your child that these ornaments are not edible!

GLUE AND PASTE

The following glue and paste recipes use a variety of ingredients and methods. Choose the one that best suits your project. For variety, add food coloring before using. Store all glues and pastes in airtight containers in the refrigerator.

Glue
¾ cup water
2 tablespoons corn syrup
1 teaspoon white vinegar
Small saucepan
Small bowl
2 tablespoons cornstarch
¾ cup cold water

Mix water, corn syrup, and vinegar in saucepan. Bring to a full, rolling boil. In bowl, mix cornstarch with cold water. Add this mixture slowly to the hot mixture, stirring constantly until the mixture returns to a boil. Boil for 1 minute, then remove from heat. When cooled, pour into another container and let stand overnight before using.

Homemade Paste

½ cup flour
Cold water
Saucepan
Food coloring (optional)

Add cold water to flour until mixture is as thick as cream. Simmer and stir in saucepan for 5 minutes. Add a few drops of food coloring, if desired. This wet, messy paste takes a while to dry.

Papier-Mâché Paste

1 cup water
¼ cup flour
5 cups lightly boiling water
Large saucepan

Mix flour into 1 cup water until mixture is thin and runny. Stir this mixture into lightly boiling water. Gently boil and stir 2–3 minutes. Cool before using.

No-Cook Paste
Bowl
½ cup flour
Water
Salt

In bowl, mix flour with enough water to make a mixture that's gooey, but not runny. Add a pinch of salt; stir.

DECORATIONS

Use the following recipes to make decorative materials for use in various art and craft projects.

Colorful Creative Salt
½ cup salt
5–6 drops food coloring
Microwave and microwave-safe container or wax paper

Add food coloring to salt and stir well. Cook in microwave 1–2 minutes or spread on wax paper and let dry. Store in airtight container. Use as glitter.

Pasta Dye

½ cup rubbing alcohol
Food coloring
Dry pasta
Newspaper
Wax paper

Mix alcohol and food coloring in a bowl. Add small amounts of dry pasta to the liquid and gently mix. The larger the pasta, the longer it will take to absorb the color. Dry on newspapers covered with wax paper. Remind your child that pasta dyed with this recipe is not for eating; it's only for art projects!

Egg Dye

Small bowls or cups
¼ teaspoon food coloring per container
¾ cup hot water per container
1 tablespoon white vinegar per container

Measure all liquids into bowl or cup and mix. Use a different color in each container. Soak eggs in dye until they reach the desired shades.

Ornamental Frosting

3 egg whites
1 teaspoon cream of tartar
Bowl
Eggbeater
1 pound powdered sugar (about 4 cups), sifted
Damp cloth

Beat egg whites with cream of tartar in bowl until stiff peaks form. Add sugar and continue beating until mixture is thick and holds its shape. Cover bowl with damp cloth when not in use. This frosting can be made from several hours to a day before use. It makes a great glue for gingerbread houses and other edible works of art. Store in an airtight container in the refrigerator.

Appendix B

Crazy Can Activities

The following activities are suitable for a toddler Crazy Can (see Chapter 1). These activities require no special materials or time-consuming preparation or cleanup, and they need only a minimal amount of adult participation. Some of these activities require a little advance planning, such as having a collection of nuts and bolts on hand for Nuts and Bolts or preparing a craft carton for Cartons of Fun. A Crazy Can will provide you with an instant remedy when things start to get crazy or when there's just "nothing to do." (The number following each activity refers to the page on which it is found.)

Appendix C

Best Toys for Babies and Toddlers

If your child is less than one year old, she probably has not yet amassed a big collection of toys. After a few birthdays and holiday celebrations, however, she will likely have more toys than you ever dreamed possible! It's a good idea to think ahead about the kinds of toys you want to invest in. There are a lot of toys out there, and more are coming out all the time. Some are worth the money they cost, while others definitely aren't.

When choosing toys for children, look for items that can be used in more than one way, that have stood the test of time, and that may be enjoyed through many years of childhood. The toys listed in this appendix meet all these criteria and are worth every penny.

For storage, try to stay away from toy boxes, which take up a lot of space and aren't particularly useful for organizing. (We have two toy boxes, lovingly handmade by Grandpa, that we use for stuffed animals and dress-up clothes.) Store items with many pieces in stackable, transparent plastic containers with lids. These fit well in closets or on shelves. Flat containers are also practical, as they slide easily under beds, utilizing otherwise wasted space. Storing toys in smaller containers instead of a toy box keeps pieces from getting mixed up (provided you don't allow your child to take out all the containers at once) and helps children develop organizational skills.

Other ideas for making the best use of toys include establishing a toy rotation or implementing a toy exchange with friends. See Chapter 1 for details.

The book *What to Expect the Toddler Years* by Arlene Eisenberg, Heidi E. Markoff, and Sandee E. Hathaway includes a great list called "Toys for Tots Early in the Second Year." The list is organized according to skills the toys help develop. Most of our family favorites are included in this list, so I have organized my recommendations in somewhat the same way. Many toys help develop more than one skill, but for simplicity's sake, I have avoided duplications.

Toys that help build fine motor skills (many also encourage discovery and interest in the physical world):

beads	nesting toys	spools
blocks	sandbox and sand toys	stacking toys
boxes	shape sorters	water toys
containers	simple wooden jigsaw puzzles	

Toys that help build gross motor skills:

balls	push toys	slides
pull toys	riding toys	swings

Toys that stimulate imagination (many also encourage learning about the grown-up world):

books	fake food	stuffed animals
building toys	kitchen accessories	tea sets
doll furniture	puppets	toy cars
dolls	shopping carts	toy telephones
dress-up clothes		

Toys that stimulate creativity (basic craft supplies):

child-safe scissors	markers	paper
coloring books	paint	playdough
crayons	paintbrushes	sponges
glue		

Toys that encourage musical play:

cassette tapes	maracas	tambourines
drums	simple keyboards	xylophones
	sturdy cassette player	

Appendix D

Best Books for Babies and Toddlers

This list of seventy authors and their books is in no way complete. Each author may have written many titles, of which only one or two are included here. Many great children's authors and books have not been included—not because they are not worthy, but because to include them all would require another volume! This list includes books and authors that are recommended by experts in the field of children's literature. Our family has read and enjoyed many of these books over the years.

The best way to learn which books your child enjoys is to read children's books—lots of them. Read not only award-winners, but also award-losers. (Some of the best-loved books are runners-up!) Read books about children's books, too. My favorite such books, ones upon which I have relied for many years, are listed in Appendix E.

Make the children's room of your library your second home. Get to know the librarians and ask for their recommendations. The most popular books are usually checked out as soon as they are returned, so reserve them if you can. If you have access to a computer, you can often reserve books from home. This service is a lifesaver for those who visit the library with infants and toddlers! If this service is not available to you, visit the library one afternoon or evening without toddlers in tow and spend some time getting to know the best in children's books, both old and new.

Ahlberg, Janet and Allan. *The Baby's Catalogue; Peek-A-Boo.*

Bang, Molly. *Ten, Nine, Eight; Yellow Ball.*

Becker, Bonny. *The Quiet Way Home.*

Brown, Margaret Wise. *Big Red Barn; Goodnight Moon; The Runaway Bunny.*

Bruna, Dick. *Dick Bruna's Animal Book; I Can Count; I Can Dress Myself;* Miffy series; *My Shirt is White.*

Burningham, John. *Mr. Gumpy's Outing.*

Carle, Eric. *My Very First Book of Colors; The Very Busy Spider; The Very Hungry Caterpillar.*

Carlstrom, Nancy White. *Jesse Bear, What Will You Wear?*

Carter, Noelle and David. *I'm a Little Mouse: A Pat and Play Book.*

Cooke, Trish. *So Much.*

Cooney, Barbara (illustrator). *Chanticleer and the Fox.*

Cousins, Lucy (illustrator). *The Little Dog Laughed: And Other Nursery Rhymes from Mother Goose.*

Crews, Donald. *Freight Train; Truck.*

De Angeli, Marguerite (illustrator). *Book of Nursery and Mother Goose Rhymes.*

De Regniers, Beatrice Schenk. *May I Bring a Friend?*

Demarest, Chris L. *My Blue Boat.*

dePaola, Tomie. *Charlie Needs a Cloak; Pancakes for Breakfast.*

Dunn, Judy. *The Little Rabbit.*

Eastman, Philip D. *Are You My Mother?*

Eichenberg, Fritz. *Ape in a Cape: An Alphabet of Odd Animals; Dancing in the Moon.*

Ets, Marie Hall. *In the Forest; Gilberto and the Wind; Play with Me.*

Flack, Marjorie. Angus series; *Ask Mister Bear; Walter the Lazy Mouse.*

Freeman, Don. *Corduroy; The Chalk Box Story.*

Fujikawa, Gyo. *Let's Eat; Puppies, Pussycats and Other Friends.*

Ga'g, Wanda. *The ABC Bunny.*

Galdone, Paul (illustrator). *The Little Red Hen; The Monkey and the Crocodile: A Jataka Tale from India; Old Mother Hubbard and Her Dog; Old Woman and Her Pig.*

Gilham, Bill. *The First Words Picture Book.*

Goudey, Alice. *The Day We Saw the Sun Come Up.*

Gramatky, Hardie. *Little Toot.*

Greenaway, Kate. *A Apple Pie*.

Hill, Eric. Spot series.

Hoban, Tana. *Circles, Triangles, and Squares; Is It Red? Is It Yellow? Is It Blue?; Push, Pull, Empty, Full*.

Hughes, Shirley. *Bathwater's Hot; Noisy; Two Shoes, New Shoes; When We Went to the Park*.

Jam, Teddy. *Night Cars*.

Johnson, Crockett. *Harold and the Purple Crayon*.

Keats, Ezra Jack. *Peter's Chair; The Snowy Day*.

Kraus, Robert. *Whose Mouse Are You?*

Krauss, Ruth. *Bears; The Carrot Seed; The Happy Day; A Hole Is to Dig: A First Book of First Definitions; You're Just What I Need* (formerly titled *The Bundle Book*).

Lansky, Bruce. *The New Adventures of Mother Goose: Gentle Rhymes for Happy Times*.

Lionni, Leo. *Frederick; Fish is Fish; Swimmy*.

Martin, Bill Jr. *Brown Bear, Brown Bear, What Do You See?; Chicka, Chicka, Boom, Boom*.

McCloskey, Robert. *Blueberries for Sal*.

McMillan, Bruce. *Here a Chick, There a Chick*.

Ormerod, Jan. *101 Things to Do with a Baby*.

Oxenbury, Helen. *Helen Oxenbury's ABC of Things; Tom and Pippo series*.

Parish, Peggy. *I Can! Can You?*

Payne, Emmy. *Katy No-Pocket.*

Pienkowski, Jan. *ABC; Colors; Numbers; Shapes.*

Piper, Watty. *The Little Engine That Could.*

Potter, Beatrix. *The Complete Adventures of Peter Rabbit.*

Ransom, Candice F. *The Big Green Pocketbook.*

Reid, Barbara. Zoe series.

Rey, H. A. *Curious George.*

Rockwell, Anne F. *Come to Town.*

Rosen, Michael. *We're Going on a Bear Hunt.*

Scarry, Richard. *Early Bird; Richard Scarry's Please and Thank You Book; Best Word Book; Richard Scarry's Cars and Trucks and Things That Go.*

Sendak, Maurice. *Alligators All Around.*

Slobodkina, Esphyr. *Caps for Sale: A Tale of a Peddler, Some Monkeys and Their Monkey Business.*

Spier, Peter. *Big Trucks, Little Trucks; Fast Cars, Slow Cars; Fast-Slow High-Low; Here Come the Fire Trucks; Noah's Ark; Trucks that Dig and Dump.*

Tafuri, Nancy. *Early Morning in the Barn; Have You Seen My Duckling?; Two New Sneakers; One Wet Jacket.*

Tresselt, Alvin. *White Snow, Bright Snow.*

Tudor, Tasha. *"A" Is for Annabelle*.

Waddell, Martin. *Owl Babies*.

Wells, Rosemary. Max series.

Wildsmith, Brian. *Wild Animals; Brian Wildsmith 1, 2, 3*.

Williams, Garth. *The Chicken Book*.

Williams, Vera B. *"More More More," Said the Baby*.

Wood, Audrey. *The Napping House*.

Zion, Gene. *Harry the Dirty Dog*.

Zolotow, Charlotte. *The Sleepy Book; Big Sister and Little Sister; Some Things Go Together; William's Doll*.

Appendix E

Resources

Very few ideas in this world are truly original; that is, no matter how new or unique an idea may seem, someone somewhere has probably had it before. Many of the ideas in this book have appeared in print elsewhere, and many of them you have probably seen, heard about, or tried yourself. I have included in this book only the very best ideas for toddlers—the ones that are the most fun as well as the most practical. These ideas were gleaned from a combination of personal experience, contributions from friends and family, and information gathered from the books listed below.

Catlin, Cynthia. *Toddlers Together: The Complete Planning Guide for a Toddler Curriculum.* Beltsville, MD: Gryphon House, 1994.

Charner, Kathy, ed. *The Giant Encyclopedia of Theme Activities for Children 2 to 5.* Beltsville, MD: Gryphon House, 1993.

Dexter, Sandi. *Joyful Play with Toddlers: Recipes for Fun with Odds and Ends.* Seattle: Parenting Press, 1995.

Eisenberg, Arlene, Heidi E. Markoff, and Sandee E. Hathaway. *What to Expect the Toddler Years.* New York: Workman Publishing Company, 1994.

Ellison, Sheila, and Judith Gray. *365 Days of Baby Love: Playing, Growing and Exploring with Babies from Birth to Age 2.* Naperville, IL: Sourcebooks, 1996.

Ellison, Sheila, and Judith Gray. *365 Days of Creative Play: For Children Two Years and Up.* Naperville, IL: Sourcebooks, 1995.

Ellison, Sheila, and Judith Gray. *365 Foods Kids Love to Eat.* Naperville, IL: Sourcebooks, 1995.

Gilbert, Labritta. *Do Touch: Instant, Easy Hands-On Learning Experiences for Young Children.* Beltsville, MD: Gryphon House, 1989.

Haas, Carolyn Buhai. *Look at Me: Creative Learning Activities for Babies and Toddlers.* Chicago: Chicago Review Press, 1987.

Hunt, Gladys. *Honey for a Child's Heart: The Imaginative Use of Books in Family Life.* 3rd ed. Grand Rapids, MI: Zondervan Publishing House, 1989.

Jones, Claudia. *Parents are Teachers, Too: Enriching Your Child's First Six Years.* Charlotte, VT: Williamson Publishing Company, 1988.

Jones, Maggie. *Understanding Your Child through Play.* Toronto: Stoddart Publishing Company, 1989.

Kohl, Mary Ann F. *Preschool Art: It's the Process, Not the Product.* Beltsville, MD: Gryphon House, 1994.

Landsberg, Michele. *Reading for the Love of It: Best Books for Young Readers*. Upper Saddle River, NJ: Prentice Hall, 1987.

Lansky, Vicky. *Feed Me! I'm Yours*. Minnetonka, MN: Meadowbrook Press, 1974.

Leach, Penelope. *Your Baby and Child: From Birth to Age Five*. New York: Alfred A. Knopf, 1990.

Martin, Elaine. *The Baby Games: The Joyful Guide to Child's Play from Birth to Three Years*. Toronto: Stoddart Publishing Company, 1988.

Matterson, Elizabeth. *Games for the Very Young*. American Heritage Press, New York: 1969.

Mayesky, Mary. *Creative Activities for Young Children*. 4th ed. Albany: Delmar Publishers, 1990.

Miller, Karen. *More Things to Do with Toddlers and Twos*. Chelsea, MA: Telshare Publishing, 1990.

Miller, Karen. *Things to Do with Toddlers and Twos*. Chelsea, MA: Telshare Publishing, 1984.

Pfiffners, George. *Earth-Friendly Toys: How to Make Fabulous Toys and Games from Reusable Objects*. John Wiley and Sons, 1994.

Reitzes, Fretta, and Beth Teitelman. *Wonderplay: Interactive and Developmental Games, Crafts, and Creative Activities for Infants, Toddlers, and Preschoolers*. Philadelphia: Running Press, 1995.

Rossi, Mary Jane Mangini. *Read to Me! Teach Me!* Wauwatosa, WI: American Baby Books, 1982.

Silberg, Jackie. *Games to Play with Toddlers.* Beltsville, MD: Gryphon House, 1993.

Silberg, Jackie. *Games to Play with Two Year Olds.* Beltsville, MD: Gryphon House, 1994.

Spencer, Zane. *One Hundred Fifty Plus! Games and Activities for Early Childhood.* Belmont, CA: Lake Publishers, 1976.

Suid, Anna. *Holiday Crafts.* Palo Alto, CA: Monday Morning Books, 1985.

Trelease, Jim. *The Read-Aloud Handbook.* 4th ed. New York: Penguin Books, 1995.

Warren, Jean. *1-2-3 Art.* Everett, WA: Warren Publishing House, 1985.

Zaslavsky, Claudia. *Preparing Young Children for Math.* New York: Schocken Books, 1979.

The United States General Services Administration offers many free and low-cost federal publications on learning activities and parenting. For a free catalog write to:
Consumer Information Center-2C
P.O. Box 100
Pueblo, Colorado 81002

Index

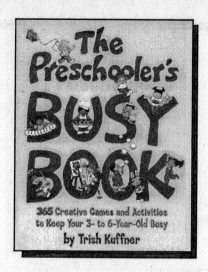

365 Creative Games and Activities to Keep Your 3- to 6-Year-Old Busy
by Trish Kuffner

The Preschooler's Busy Book

by Trish Kuffner

This book contains 365 activities (one for each day of the year) for three- to six-year-olds using things found around the home. It shows parents and day-care providers how to:

- Prevent boredom during even the longest stretches of bad weather, with ideas for indoor play, kitchen activities, and arts and crafts projects;

- Save money by making your own paints, playdough, craft clays, glue, paste, and other arts and crafts supplies;

- Stimulate a child's natural curiosity with fun reading, math, and science activities;

- And much, much more!

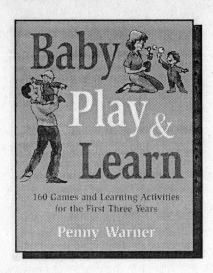

Baby Play & Learn

by Penny Warner

Child development expert Penny Warner offers 160 ideas for games and activities that will provide hours of developmental learning opportunities and fun for babies. *Baby Play & Learn* includes:

- A bulleted list of skills that babies learn through each type of play;
- Step-by-step instructions for each game and activity;
- Illustrations demonstrating how to play many of the games.

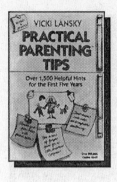

Practical Parenting Tips

by Vicki Lansky

Here's the #1-selling collection of helpful hints for parents with babies and small children. It contains over 1,500 parent-tested tips for dealing with diaper rash, nighttime crying, toilet training, temper tantrums, and traveling with tots. It will help parents save time, trouble, and money.

Feed Me! I'm Yours

by Vicki Lansky

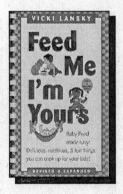

Now expanded, updated, and revised for the '90s! This best-selling baby and toddler food cookbook has sold millions of copies. It's a must-have book for all new parents. It contains more than 200 child-tested recipes and is comb-bound for easy use.

"A well-written, homorous combination cookbook and advice book that makes the job of parenting a lot easier and enjoyable."
—*Milwaukee Journal*

Gentle Discipline
by Dawn Lighter, M.A.

Dawn Lighter has written a breakthrough book that will change the way parents think about and practice discipline. Most parents think of discipline as something to do after children misbehave. Lighter's book provides 50 simple, effective ways to teach children good behavior—so they won't misbehave.

Discipline without Shouting or Spanking
by Jerry Wyckoff, Ph.D. and Barbara C. Unell

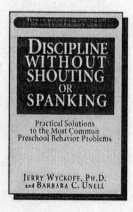

Do you know all the theories about child rearing but still have trouble coping with some of your child's misbehavior? You'll love this book! It covers the 30 most common forms of misbehavior, from whining to throwing temper tantrums. You'll find clear, practical advice on what to do, what not to do, and how to prevent each problem from recurring.

Child Care A to Z
by Dr. Richard C. Woolfson

This easy-to-understand reference contains up-to-date information on 170 topics that every parent needs to know. It is organized alphabetically to help parents find answers to questions about their child's physical, emotional, and intellectual development. Dr. Woolfson is known as the Dr. Spock of the United Kingdom, and his child-care experience is now available to American parents.

How to Read Your Child Like a Book
by Lynn Weiss, Ph.D.

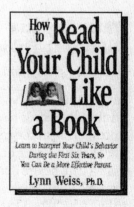

This is the first book that helps parents interpret their child's behavior by teaching parents what their child is thinking. Dr. Lynn Weiss, a nationally recognized expert on child development, explains 50 different behaviors of young children from birth to age 6 to give parents new insight into such behaviors as boundary testing, selfishness, and temper tantrums.

Moms Say the Funniest Things!

by Bruce Lansky

Lansky has collected moms' most popular lines for dealing with "emergencies" like getting the kids out of bed, cleaned, dressed, to school, to the dinner table, undressed, and back to bed. It includes all-time winners like "Put on clean underwear—you never know when you'll be in an accident" and "If God had wanted you to fool around, He would have written the 'Ten Suggestions.'" A fun gift for mom!

Dads Say the Dumbest Things!

by Bruce Lansky and K. L. Jones

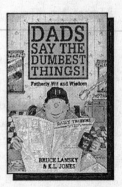

Lansky and Jones have collected all the greatest lines dads have ever used to get kids to stop fighting in the car, feed the pet, turn off the TV while doing homework, and get home from a date before curfew. It includes winners like "What do you want a pet for—you've got a sister" and "When I said 'feed the goldfish,' I didn't mean feed them to the cat." A fun gift for dad!

"Mary McBride is the undiscovered Bombeck"
—JOAN RIVERS

Grandma Knows Best, But No One Ever Listens!

Hilarious helpful hints for grandmas.

Mary McBride

FOREWORD BY PHYLLIS DILLER

Grandma Knows Best, But No One Ever Listens!

by Mary McBride

McBride offers much-needed advice for new grandmas on how to:

- Show baby photos to anyone at any time;
- Get out of baby-sitting or, if stuck, "housebreak" the kids before they wreck the house;
- Advise the daughter-in-law without being banned from her home.

The perfect gift for Grandma. Phyllis Diller says it's "harder to put down than a new grandchild."

Also from Meadowbrook Press

◆ *Healthy Food for Healthy Kids*
A practical guide to selecting and preparing healthy meals for kids and teaching healthy attitudes toward food. More than just a cookbook, this is a user-friendly book with real-world advice for parents who want their children to eat better.

◆ *Parent-Tested Ways to Grow Your Child's Confidence*
With 150 tested ideas designed to enhance your child's self-confidence, you'll discover great ways to share enjoyable moments together, teach important skills, celebrate special occasions, encourage creativity, and recognize achievements.

◆ *Play and Learn*
Baby Play and Learn and *Preschooler Play and Learn*, from child-development expert Penny Warner, offer ideas for games and activities that will provide hours of developmental learning opportunities and fun for babies and young children. Each book contains step-by-step instructions, illustrations, and bulleted lists of skills your child will learn through play activities.

**We offer many more titles written to delight, inform, and entertain.
To order books with a credit card or browse our full
selection of titles, visit our web site at:**

www.meadowbrookpress.com

or call toll-free to place an order, request a free catalog, or ask a question:

1-800-338-2232

Meadowbrook Press • 5451 Smetana Drive • Minnetonka, MN • 55343